THOROUGHLY MODERN PATRIOT

AUSTRALIA, THE MONARCHY AND A FAIR FIGHT

SEAN JACOBS

Connor Court Publishing

Thoroughly Modern Patriot: Australia, the Monarchy and a Fair Fight
by Sean Jacobs

Published by Connor Court Publishing Pty Ltd

Copyright © Sean Jacobs, 2022

ALL RIGHTS RESERVED. This book contains material protected under International and Federal Copyright Laws and Treaties. Any unauthorised reprint or use of this material is prohibited. No part of this book may be reproduced or transmitted in any form or by any means, electronic or mechanical, including photocopying, recording, or by any information storage and retrieval system without express written permission from the publisher.

PO Box 7257
Redland Bay QLD 4165
sales@connorcourt.com
www.connorcourt.com

ISBN: 9781922449856

Cover design by Maya Walker

Printed in Australia

Dedicated to my wonderful parents Greg and Martha

Also by Sean Jacobs

Winners Don't Cheat:
Advice for young Australians from a young Australian (2018).

Neville Bonner:
Australia's first Indigenous Parliamentarian (2020).

Author's Note

I've tried to write these pages with utility – in a way that's the *most* accessible to the *most* number of people. Being neither an academic historian or legal expert, I've attempted to apply everyday terms for interested readers without being careless. In some parts, for example, I've referred to 'Australia' before formal federation, when it's clear that 'the colonies' might be more accurate. At times I also lump Australian 'republican lobbyists' and 'republicans' into the same camp when I know this may not be entirely fair. I've tried to be careful here – not only for friends in the republic movement but also to fairly capture their ideas. And I swap between 'constitutional monarchy', 'the monarchy' and 'the Crown' in a way that may alarm staunch monarchists or historians. But I suspect most won't be too offended or confused. Again – none of this is due to carelessness. My primary hope is to bring this fascinating debate to a wider number of people, while not losing the integrity of the arguments – including my own.

A Short Note On The Future

There's a memorable story of a man strolling through a park and, upon seeing a portrait painter, stops to get his profile painted. After sitting for five minutes the artist gives him his portrait and asks for his payment – $50. Although the job is quite good, the man is slightly perplexed. 'But it only took you five minutes?' he asks. 'Five minutes,' the artist replies, 'and twenty years'.

It's a decent parable – one that explains, in simple terms, the concept of hidden costs. There are many examples of not just hidden costs but 'hidden complexities' in modern Australia. A five-year old speaking to their toy Barbie, for example, can ask a question and receive an automated response in under a second. Impressive. But especially impressive when considering the five-year old's voice has travelled halfway around the world to ToyTalk servers, and the response algorithmically selected from 8,000 lines of dialogue.

Aside from toys, companies work tirelessly to develop, package and deliver products to supermarket shelves at competitive prices. Flat pack furniture travels across the planet to be conveniently assembled in our living rooms and, by using plastic instead of metals, reduces environmental burden.

Thanks to responsive creativity in the marketplace, the

average automobile today is actually 99 percent cleaner than it was in the 1970s. Global financial services, like taking money out of an ATM, enlist a complex series of global interactions that take place in a simple matter of seconds. Even in 1993, in Malcolm Turnbull's *The Reluctant Republic*, Turnbull wrote that "getting rid of a Governor-General is just a matter of the Prime Minister sending a fax to Buckingham Palace".[1] This task – if we'd ever want to perform it – could now be done on a mobile phone.

These summits of innovation, and great leaps forward, make us enthusiastic about the future. But what about the innovation of our institutions? Are they built to last, and can we rely on them to meet the challenges of our time, and of tomorrow?

We often forget that our formal institutions – the Australian Constitution, Westminster legislatures in our states and territories, Governors and Governors-General, our 'courts, clerks and contracts' – also have hidden costs. All have hidden complexities, transplanted from cold wet islands in the North Atlantic to dry and dusty Australian land.

But even before our formal institutions touched down on Indigenous Australian soil these institutions, in themselves, were built on centuries of difficulty, and trial and error. 'Hidden costs' were bloody, difficult and miserable, contrasting with the picture of modern convenience we have in front of us today. There were at least nine major English civil wars, for example, during the period from the Norman Conquest to the Glorious Revolution, during which time the idea of parliament slowly developed. But this wasn't 'parliament' that would pass public expectations today. Looking back, even 1800s Australian representative democracy is very different from our modern state and federal legislatures.

What I hope to show in these pages is that being proud of our institutions – or in this case being a 'monarchist' – doesn't mean staying stuck in the past. Or so wedded to history as to be unmoved by current and future challenges.

Australians, after all, are naturally forward looking. But in a unique way. When thinking about the future, we apparently tend to be instinctively cautious about what Australian pollster Mark Textor calls "the vision thing".[2] "It's not vision," Textor famously noted, "it's the horizon that people seek".

It can be a neat way to think about things. Our institutions provide a vision and a safe space to pursue our lives. But they're not our horizon.

A horizon is something we shape for ourselves. A rule of law, for example, means we're protected from howling mobs. But deciding whether to be in the mob or not is up to us. Private property offers us protection for what we own. But it's also a door to close on enemies and, when we want, swing open to friends. We can vote for whoever we like and join the political parties of our choosing. A free press helps a free society. And our Constitution, rather than notes on a passing scene, keeps politicians in check and remains sturdy and difficult to change.

Being grateful for these things doesn't mean that reform is over. When businesses seek relief from having to produce 22,000 page environmental impact statements, for example, or residents from filling out a 29 page form to hold a small street party, it's clear there's more work to be done.

But these point to challenges *in* the arena but not *of* the arena. Republican lobbyists often confuse the two. Political, economic, environmental and social challenges require political, economic, environmental and social solutions. A republic shouldn't be a solution looking for a problem.

So if we look to a horizon what shape would it take? As a proud constitutional monarchy, what would a future Australia look like?

I believe it's an Australia that has a renewed sense of cultural confidence. Where we can celebrate patriotism without flamboyance or resentment but with gratitude and humility. A future not crammed with endless dreaming but *practical* people wanting to fix *practical* problems. Communities striving for equality of opportunity. Of governments steadied by the will of the people and seeking to get the big things right. And continuing to look within but also to our region for our most tenacious wins.

And all of this, as we know, comes from a potent mix of the 'top down' and the 'bottom up' – not just good institutions but good people.

Preface

It was after visiting Vietnam in my early thirties – not *too* long ago – that I decided to finally finish Graham Greene's 1956 classic *The Quiet American*. Set during the First Indo-China War (1946-1954), and prior to America's injection into what we now know as 'the Vietnam War', the novel's main characters are Fowler – a self-exiled and clapped out British journalist – and Pyle – a young, idealistic and thinly disguised American CIA agent.

Fowler does not like what he sees in Pyle roaming the streets of Saigon – overconfidence, slim self-awareness and a belief that complex problems can be solved by American know-how.

I didn't find the book great. But it remains a classic, unsurprisingly emerging every now and then as a 'tut tut' toward American hubris in world affairs. "For those today seeking to understand how the United States blundered so badly in Iraq and Afghanistan," wrote former U.S. Army Colonel Andrew Bacevich in 2009, "*The Quiet American* remains an essential text".[1]

But I found it a more useful prompt in slightly more humbled foreign settings – Australia's perception in Asia

– where it's claimed our image has been sharpened by a similar hubris and arrogance. This is an area where we have, according to some, failed to use our 'soft power' wisely while suffering a self-deception of importance.

"There is a significant gap between Australians' self image and views of Australia in the region," writes one well-known Australian commentator. As he continues:

> We tend to regard our country as a stable, prosperous, liberal democracy that boasts cultural harmony and enjoys healthy respect from other nations. Arguably, this isn't always the way our neighbours regard us. There remains a perception of a lingering racism tied to the old White Australia. Some countries appear to treat us largely with indifference, contrary to our own sense of regional importance.[2]

I suspect some Australians would agree with these gentle criticisms. But I'd expect many more – in facts *lots* more – wouldn't. I see three main reasons.

First, the comments clearly undermine the remarkable success of Australia's institutions – our 'courts, clerks and contracts' but also our families and communities – in building social cohesion. Australian history, if anything, is filled with examples of pragmatism at the expense of excessive feelings of regional importance. Second, the words manufacture a 'lingering racism' that, today, simply doesn't exist – at least not in a way that defines our entire geostrategic relationship with neighbours near and far. And third, these comments offer an easy 'gateway drug' to not only discredit *ourselves* but 'change' the very things that have given Australia its appeal – our stable, prosperous, liberal democracy.

Granted, there's a lot to take issue with in *one* statement from *one* commentator. But I offer it here because it's casual arguments like these that can overlook past successes, hasten democratic impatience, grow into the thinking of our academic, business and media institutions, and drive careless calls for change.

This short book is a gentle, and I hope appealing, pause to this trend. It is a counteroffer to the overriding solution to our modern lack of democratic energy – an Australian republic.

The debate over an Australian republic is one of the seismic issues of our time. It deserves great consideration – encompassing the journey we've been on, how young we still are, and how special it is to remain part of symbol that goes back over 800 hundred years, and touches a genuinely diverse 53 states and 2.4 billion people.

The fact Australia is a constitutional monarchy isn't likely to be on the minds of many Australians. It won't, after all, have much to do with how fast we drive down the road. Or how much tax we pay.

But it does speak to things that all Australians possess some instinct for – our proud history and civic life, the rights and responsibilities we enjoy, the stability and responsible government we expect, and the expectations we place upon on each other as citizens.

A monarchy has been important to Australia because it has reminded us of symbols above politics. It side steps the complications of modern republics, presidents, shutdowns and logjam. And, even as a young nation, it recognises our independence and capacity to stand on our own two feet.

How else could Australia defend itself, with little help from Britain, in fierce jungle fighting in Papua New Guinea (PNG) and the Pacific Islands? How else could we be such a stable magnet for the region, where a majority of new Australians to our major cities are now Asian born? And how, despite our egalitarian scepticism for political leaders, could we maintain such respect for the Office of the Governor-General, and Queen Elizabeth II?

While the Queen will eventually pass, a previous generation of Australians have shown us that respect follows the *institution* more than the *individual*. The Queen's decades of commitment have drawn on Queen Victoria's timeless lessons from the previous century – duty, service and acknowledging change.

Queen Elizabeth's hereditary example in our time has not been of ensconced privilege but unbroken continuity – a phenomenon built to last in an age of short-termism. All royals, we should expect, will follow similar lines of tradition, albeit under more ever-intrusive modern media scrutiny, but constantly tilting conventions to modern expectations. All of us commend these ideals of continuity because we see this appeal in ourselves. And in our families. And in our communities.

Australians are fortunate to possess an institutional attachment to the English Crown. And it'd be to Australia's disappointment – our disadvantage – if we were to break away, generating greater problems than the many we wish to solve in our time.

1

A Lazy Cosmopolitan

I had lost about a litre of sweat. Cricket pads and batting gloves hugged my body as I stood shirtless in the practice nets. The harsh Fijian sun roasted my exposed torso as I pretended to be a decent cricket batsman.

Shirtless cricket isn't common in Australia but, in the South Pacific, incessant heat relaxes decorum. I was in my early twenties and spending a year in Fiji as part of the Australian Youth Ambassadors for Development Program. Over the last two decades this largely unknown program – administered by the Australian Government – has placed many young Australians throughout the region, working across governance, health, education and civil society sectors, with the ultimate aim of building people to people links with some of our closest neighbours. It has seen thousands of young Australians contributing to public service and adding to Australia's regional profile.

Although volunteering to help run Fiji Swimming, in my spare time, when not indulging in cold Fijian beers, I'd joined a local cricket side. On this hot Suva afternoon, I was practicing cricket with a handful of local enthusiasts, which included a devoted mix of Aussies, Fijians, Indians, Iranians, Pakistanis, and other expatriates.

Sport is unifying and cricket – much like the old lumbering British Empire – brings together a pretty interesting bunch of people. After England's 2019 Cricket World Cup victory, it was observed that England's tie-breaking 'super over' was bowled by Barbadian-born Jofra Archer and helped won by teammates with names like Adil Rashid. "So what's English?" asked *The UK Spectator* following England's world cup win, "And who's English?"[1]

While I never rose to any standout prominence in cricket, I at least recognised that being *good* required a mastery of strokes, measured emphasis and an ability to read the game. "How do the pros hit it so well mate?" I asked my Australian friend, Dave Kachor, hoping for some tips as I retired in sweat-soaked pads and gloves. After a few hand gestures and a medley of cricket terms he finally summed it up to me. "It's really about having the confidence to know yourself".

While not the most flawless anecdote, it is a short piece of advice that has stayed with me. One feature of many decent and everyday Australians I've met, and those I've studied closely, is that they know themselves tremendously well. They discharge their responsibilities by working hard, serving those around them, building good families and creating strong communities. Strengths, weaknesses, moments of greatness, and passages of hardship, clearly shape how we view the world, encounter circumstances, acknowledge our flaws and build confidence when required.

I can't help but think that, at least in part, nations are no different. Knowing ourselves means studying our history and acknowledging wrong turns. But it ultimately means looking at the *best* elements of our past to get the *best* out of ourselves.

Proactively Positive

In pivoting from cricket to the issue of an Australian republic, I admit to being a John Howard tragic. I cite the former Prime Minister too excessively at times. But he makes far too many important points worth repeating, even for our current times. In 1996 Howard said, only months after coming to office, that:

> ... over the years different politicians have used their own interpretations of the history of their country and indeed the history of the world, those of who've establish a particular view of political legitimacy. And it's our responsibility to ensure that Australians of future generations have a comprehensive, factually based, objective view of the history of this country, not coloured unduly by one or other interpretation, but reflecting an *emphatically positive view* of what this country has achieved and particularly since the Federation in 1901.[2] [italics mine]

I believe Howard is right – we need to be 'emphatically positive' about our past. But, like many others, I've been in too many conversations where to talk in such a way invites immediate disapproval. For some critics, the dispossession of Indigenous Australians, the insularity of the White Australia Policy, or the rigid social attitudes of previous eras, tempers growing too fond of our historical achievements.

Australians, I feel, should be proud of our past. The monarchy-republic debate offers us a chance to be clear-eyed about this, acknowledging where we've fallen short of our ideals, but also dispelling myths of past deficits and a rare chance to see our constitutional monarchy as a source of renewal.

Indeed, why I find this debate so fascinating is because we're told that an Australian republic, or more specifically an Australian President, offers us a slipstream to correct the past and put us on more noble footing. As then-prime minister Paul Keating said in 1995, in the speech that 'started it all' for the modern republic:

> An Australian Head of State can embody our modern aspirations – our cultural diversity, our evolving partnerships with Asia and the Pacific, our quest for reconciliation with Aboriginal Australians, our ambition to create a society in which women have equal opportunity, equal representation and equal rights.[3]

Despite the burial of a republic at the 1999 referendum, it is a desire far from left in the 1990s. A republic today – well into the twenty-first century – is Labor Party politics. Commanding the attention of many decent Australians, it will stay with us. And, combined with the dissatisfaction of an influential section of the Australian community, it presents real currency as a movement for change.

An Odd Advocate

In cautioning against an Australian republic, I admit, I don't look like your typical constitutional monarchist. I have carefully learned over the years that appearance can be synonymous with assumptions about such things.

I was born in Port Moresby, PNG, to an Australian father and Papua New Guinean mother. My Australian Grandfather deployed to PNG during World War Two, flying Bristol Beaufighters against the Japanese. Not long after the war, my Papua New Guinean grandfather – from the archipelagos of New Ireland Province – formed part of the Royal Papua New Guinean Constabulary, deploying far from island life to the PNG Highlands to help keep law and order in Australia's then-colony.

PNG is a nation that, due to its cultural groupings and 900-plus languages, fascinates and excites many. But pluralism can be challenging. Over the years I have returned to PNG, not just on countless occasions to see family, but to work with the United Nations and other organisations on difficult issues around violence against women, economic empowerment, security building and political governance.

What I've learnt is that diversity can be enchanting but, without anything to tie it together, and especially strong institutions and political structures, cohesion can quickly unravel. Disagreement becomes common. Corruption corrodes years of effort. And services then rarely reach the most in need.

It goes without saying that the people of PNG don't have much. When organised politics has largely let them down, however, the British monarchy remains a symbol that restores and elevates tradition. This is important for people in a modernising world. Papua New Guineans are much more likely to be moved not by palace scandal, or labels of 'republican' or 'monarchist', but by everything that the Crown can – at its core – continue to stand for – prestige, stability, common bonds, measured tradition. To receive a knighthood – dated grandeur for some – remains a serious and appreciated honour, alongside a towering respect for Queen Elizabeth II. It's not too much of an abstraction for her Majesty to remain as PNG's Head of State – as she does in Australia and 14 other nations.

A Commonwealth Appeal

These appreciations, however, escaped a young Sean Jacobs. When very young I moved from PNG to the small middle eastern kingdom of Bahrain. It was an odd place for my brother and I – often mistaken for middle eastern boys and, Mum, with her dark complexion, either central African or Saudi Arabian. Most Bahrainis possessed an idea of Australia on a map. But PNG drew blank looks.

In Bahrain I travelled throughout East Africa, the Arabian Gulf and South Asia. With a father as an international airline pilot, I had the unique fortune of being exposed to different cultures that, rather than repelling me from western tradition, actually drew me into its orbit. Sitting cross-legged in class I can still recall my Indian, Pakistani, American, British, Egyptian and Libyan schoolmates, many also mixed-race, labouring and triumphing under a British curriculum. As in those later years playing cricket on a small island in the middle of the Pacific, there was no cultural superiority emphasised, no expressions of jingoism or gusto for the Union Jack – just a simple acknowledgement of coming together, a common pursuit, a universal set of rules and leaving any distinctions at the door.

This appeal, matched with seeing the value of institutions in PNG, enlivened the Commonwealth ideals I feel strongly about today – genuine democracy, human rights, rule of law, good governance. But no one needs exclusively mixed heritage, or to work in international aid, or to move across the planet and share classrooms with diverse peers, to see the ongoing value of distinctively British institutions and the positive impact they can continue to have in the world. We all possess instincts for common bonds, stability and to leave distinctions at the door.

Thoroughly modern patriot

In bringing this all back to our times and our current affairs it's true that, while a Howard tragic, I also greatly respect Paul Keating – a man who left school at fifteen, taking us through some of the biggest economic reforms in Australian history, deserves a great deal. Keating's ideals must also be understood and respected in the atmosphere of the times, which was the fall of the Berlin Wall and re-thinking of the instruments of state and government.

But on the issue of a republic his enthusiasm – and the desire that many have in the modern Australian republic movement – remains misguided. Australia is already culturally diverse, we have enjoyed a unique relationship with Asian and Pacific neighbours, Indigenous Australians share strong traditions with the monarchy – as in our shared system of government – while equality of opportunity, rather than equality of outcome, remains the best guarantee of a free society in a not always free world. As a constitutional monarchy, we would do well to stick to these ideals rather than run from them.

2

Something To Be Proud Of

It's hard not to be impressed at how far Australia has come from a very basic start. The first ensemble of marines and convicts – around 1200 of them on 11 ships – arrived in Sydney Cove in 1788. The journey from England to Australia, which now takes less than a day with the aid of Airbus or Boeing, then took eight months by sea. Sydney, of course, was entirely bare. No roads, bridges or buildings jammed the Sydney landscape as they do today. Dusty and miserable years lay ahead for the early convicts and settlers.

Today, over two hundred years later, and even with the impacts of COVID-19, Australia enjoys one of the highest standards of living in the world. Australia's national ethos has cascaded over generations to respect and admire courage, democracy, mateship, stamina and loyalty. We're a nation that, in step with these high ideals, asserts an egalitarian satire to ensure few get 'above their station'. Australia remains a desired destination for those not only fleeing conflict and pursing education but also for many seeking fresh starts and new horizons.

Thoroughly modern patriot

As Australians we foster a huge mix of ethnicities and cultures, but successfully rally our diversity around common institutions and the rule of law.

In all of this, however, it's worth recalling that the early Australia did not have a champion start. Life for the colony's early settlers and convicts required a raw degree of genuine grit and resilience to ward-off starvation, enliven commercial activity and overcome the timeless challenge of human affairs – managing disagreement. These early years did not tell a story of 'mythic status' but hard reality.

In the late 1780s, despite some quite decent planning, a quarter of the first settlement nearly died from starvation. Australia's hunter-gatherer Indigenous population was yet to develop largescale farming, which meant no sustained food supply. A Dutch Merchant, Abel Tasman, had touched part of Australia over a century before the First Fleet's arrival and, finding virtually nothing to trade, quickly moved on. From seeds to leg irons, everything had to be brought on the 11 ships of the First Fleet.

Critical observations were made about the tough Australian landscape. The 'rock star' botanist of his day – Joseph Banks – famously wrote in his diary as part of Cook's 1770 voyage that New Holland – then the name of the Australian continent – was the "most barren country I have seen".[1] Banks, taking meticulous samples of plants and fora, apparently even said that sheep would not thrive in New South Wales due to the unsuitable conditions.[2] A lack of navigable waterways in Australia's inland, in contrast to many other colonies, would not only prohibit agricultural activity but eventually force many settlers to rely purely on creativity and persistence in 'unlocking' the harsh outback.

To compound the colony's problems the Second Fleet, expected to bring essential supplies in 1790, suffered 278 deaths on the journey from Britain. Much-needed food was lost, puncturing hopes of resupply. For those eagerly awaiting the next wave of settlement, one can imagine the collective deflation as 124 convicts, covered in lice and too sick to move, were hauled off boats and then died. The Second Fleet carries the grim moniker 'the Death Fleet' – hardly a winning signature for the early waves of settlement.

Although Australia has a proud history of invention and innovation, the early years were also absent of what today's management consultants call 'knowledge-intensive capital'. Some of Australia's greatest inventions – the stump-jump plough or the Sunshine Harvester – took decades to emerge. "The people in the earliest colonies," writes Thomas Barlow in *The Australian Miracle*, "were almost totally devoid of any technological skills".[3] The first trained geologist didn't settle in Australia until 1839, he notes, while the first civil engineer didn't arrive until 1823. "By as late as 1850," Barlow adds, "there were still only an estimated fifty engineers out of a total European population of 400 000". This is astonishing, especially when considering art galleries, libraries, churches and other major buildings had been constructed.

Invention and innovation would be the key to overcoming Australia's harsh environment and unlocking the productive capacity of the land. At a time when we solely think of high-tech as 'innovation' – complex algorithms, for instance, or automation – it's worth recalling Australia's much less glamorous leaps forward. Wool, for example, became commercially successful only after sheep were imported and mixed in the 1790s by entrepreneur and former military man John McArthur. The application and economic value of iron ore and copper, which today make up the lion's share of Australia's mineral exports, were only realised over time. Other inventions, such as rust-resistant wheat, the Sunshine Harvester and the Ridley Stripper, not only responded to necessity but enabled Australia to grow and prosper. An Australian farmer a century ago, it's said, would feed only his family. Today an Aussie farmer feeds around 700 people.

Growing Pains

In the early years, political problems in the new colony emerged as friction grew between authority and enterprise. The 1975 dismissal of Prime Minister Gough Whitlam is seen as the most seismic political crisis in our history. But the 1808 Rum Rebellion, which in fact had little to do with rum, has remained Australia's only armed insurrection.

What was the cause? I admit I've always found this quite strange. But context helps. The fourth Governor of New South Wales – William Bligh – arrived to Australia with a mandate to reign-in the rum trade, which was monopolised by civil and military government officers. Although today it'd be strange to see Australian Defence Force personnel collecting taxes and trading alcohol, at the time such activities were common. Alcohol delivered roaring commerce and social lubrication, especially against the backdrop of some pretty ordinary settings. "Life was lame," writes Grace Karskens in *The Colony*, "incomplete without drink".[4]

Bligh, frustrating more than a few fellow sailors throughout his accomplished naval career, inevitably upset the commercial interests and status of the New South Wales Officer Corps. In particular, he struggled to tame the commercial initiatives of McArthur, eventually issuing a warrant for McArthur's arrest. Despite his role in stimulating the colony's economic prospects, McArthur's fines went 'unpaid', refusing to recognise Bligh's authority. On 26 January 1808, the Corp's Commanding Officer – Major George Johnston, whose land Bligh wanted to reclaim – arrested Bligh.

The legal system following Bligh's arrest was eventually dissolved by a replacement Governor – Lachlan Macquarie – who arrived in 1810, deporting the Corp and bringing in his own officers. Macquarie, notably, would be the first *military* officer to rule the colony. Previous Governors – Phillip, Hunter, King and

Thoroughly modern patriot

Bligh – were all distinguished naval men of the seas. Macquarie's restoration of the rule of law would set the tone for Australia's success and, with his more visionary and cosmopolitan approach to governing, push the colony into a new gear.

Although turbulent, I've always seen the Rum Rebellion as an odd symbol of the slow but measured economic progress being made in the colony. Officers were not the only agents seeking to sell goods, acquire land and pursue a life of upward mobility – convicts also began to tug the threads of prosperity. As early as 1789, two years after the first ships pulled into Sydney, the first emancipated (freed) convict was given land. Convicts in fact made up the majority of Australia's early population and it wasn't until 1828 that they became outnumbered by free men. Convicts were clearly put to work according to their skills. Roads and bridges needed to be built, and land needed to be cleared. Convicts were integral to Australia's early and ongoing economic success – not only for their generally good work ethic – but as an obvious source of cheap labour.

It's important to briefly recall here the reasons *why* convicts were being sent to Australia. In the mid to late 1700s, overcrowding was a major problem in English prisons. With the United States having won independence and no longer a prisoner destination, Britain needed new land. Property in England around this time was also viewed as "the holiest of the holies", meaning that theft was severely punished.[5] Stealing a chicken or loaf of bread, for example, could meet the harsh sanction of exile. This is not to say that all convicts were petty thieves – a few studies have shown many were "hardened criminals" and well-acquainted with crime.[6] Around 160,000 convicts were transported to Australia until the 1860s when transportation ended.

Today many of us don't realise that a number of proposals other than Australia were put forward for Britain's new convict destination, which even included Sierra Leone in East Africa. Although it's often said that Australia was simply the best 'dumping ground' for convicts, some historians have argued there was more sophistication guiding British decision-makers. Some argue, for example, that flax and timber were important and that Australia could be a source of supply. Britain, others say, was thinking about its chief competitors of the time – France and Spain – with a naval base on Australia's east coast perfect to countering competitive geostrategic ambitions.

Upwardly Mobile

While convict life in Australia could be miserable, there are two factors that show the growing continent was becoming, even then, a land of fresh starts. First, the depraved social conditions of the 1700s and early 1800s Britain didn't replicate in New South Wales or any of the new colonies. Although alcoholism was common in Sydney, it seemed little comparison to the fused misery of life in England's bulging jails or the landscape of drunkenness and vice, especially for those lower down the social order.

Compared to other colonies Australia appeared to be doing reasonably well. In contrast to other outposts like Portuguese South America, some visitors to the new colony, such as Charles Darwin, were "full of admiration" of Sydney in the 1830s.[7] "Here," he wrote in *The Voyage of the Beagle*, "in a less promising country, scores of years have done many times more than an equal number of centuries have effected in South America". It was clear that, not even forty years after the First Fleet, Australia was growing into a much more prospective environment for convicts and settlers than the global alternatives that existed at the time.

Second, a scan of the convicts who went on to 'make it' shows that, through compromise and hard work, emancipists could eventually do well in the growing colony. Through a ticket of leave, certificate of freedom, conditional pardon or an absolute pardon, a convict could secure independence – easing the burden on government – and strike out making it on their own. Over the decades, various Governors would also make efforts to provide emancipists with opportunities. A scan of notable convicts to Australia shows that many went on to become authors, merchants, architects, farmers and entrepreneurs. Not all did exceptionally well but, for those that did, the colonies were places for upward mobility.

Not all of Australia's early settlers, of course, were ex-criminals. People with wealth – property owners and 'squatters' as they came to be known – also emerged as enterprising figures. Importantly, however, and despite the distinction attached to property ownership, the English template of aristocracy didn't quite 'fit' on Australian soil. Squatters or pastoralists searching for elite status or gentry would be quickly hauled back to reality.

An Australian Equality

Australia's tough conditions, after all, required 'all hands on deck' rather than a master-servant, or 'upstairs-downstairs', arrangement. Here is the late Australian historian Geoffrey Dutton writing in his 1985 book *The Squatters*:

> The boss is the boss, certainly, but if he is any good he never asks a man to do what he cannot do himself. At work in the sheep yards, or lamb-marking, or cutting out cattle or bringing in a mob of sheep or cattle there is usually nothing in action or clothing (or use of the judicious, helpful oath) between owner and station hand. After work the owner may retire to the main house, 'Government House', but *at work everyone is in together*.[8] [italics mine]

This early sense of egalitarianism – everyone in together – remains deeply fundamental to Australians. It's an idea however that can be difficult to articulate and, to paraphrase George Orwell's assessment of the 'English mystique', trying too hard to "break it down" generally does more harm than good.⁹ It's not difficult to appreciate this fusion of rugged individualism with a sense of duty and collective responsibility. 'If one man leans on his shovel,' as the saying goes, 'everyone else must dig harder'.

Even today, from politics to business, a social handbrake still applies to anyone who elevates too far 'above their station'. References to the 'tall poppy syndrome' – a term we don't hear too much of today – isn't always intended to invoke nastiness. As a kind of 'cultural joke', it emphasises a healthy degree of self-deprecation and satire – essential ingredients for a successful society.

Good manners are also a form of egalitarianism – saying 'thank you' to the bus driver, for example, or sitting in the front of the cab. These are small but powerful examples of decent civility in modern Australia. Even in the lead up to federation, Henry Parkes – Australia's 'Father of Federation' – underlined 'manners' as one of the lynchpins of a future federation.

Egalitarianism also translates from social norms into our legal system, symbolised in a blunt, early and very clear message to early Australians – no one is above the law. In 1788, the first convict was hanged for stealing. A year later six marines were also hanged for the same offence, sending a clear message that the rule of law applied 'across the board' regardless of connection or occupation.

In fact, over decades, the rule of law consistently triumphed over whims, howling mobs or attitudes of arbitrary prejudice. Setting early 'rules of the game' weren't just important but critical for social cohesion. There are two other examples of this.

The first is the 1838 Myall Creek Massacre, where around 30 innocent Indigenous men and women were hunted and savagely killed. When first on trial the 11 perpetrators were bizarrely acquitted. 'I would never see a white man hanged,' supposedly said one juror afterward, 'for killing a black'.[10] This stunned the New South Wales Governor, George Gipps, who ordered a retrial, and the perpetrators were found guilty and hanged. For Gipps, or any other legal official, turning a blind eye in the administration of justice would've been unthinkable.

Yet the Myall Creek trial came decades after similar, smaller scale, examples of the British justice system applying on frontier Australian soil. The first prosecution concerning the killing of an Indigenous Australian was actually in 1797 – within a decade of colonial arrival. Four years later, notes Australian legal scholar David Flint, a convict by the name of John Kirby was also sentenced to death for killing a local Indigenous man.[11] These, I admit, aren't wonderful examples. But they highlight a very clear and important message – no one is above the law.

The second example of legal triumph over prejudice is the 1861 Anti-Chinese riot at Lambing Flat, New

South Wales, where tension and grievance were fuelled by the rejection of an anti-Chinese bill in the state legislature. A mob of around 3000 miners, believing more Chinese were on their way to the goldfields, rampaged through Chinese gold mining camps, forcing around 1000 Chinese workers to flee. But police and military reinforcements quickly deployed to crush the belligerents and restore law and order. Under British law, targeting innocent people, or again turning a blind eye, based on complexion or cultural heritage, was unthinkable. Indeed, the outcome at Lambing Flat was an important distinguishing feature of where Australia was heading and the nation it would become.

A Yard Glass And A Free Society

Taking a step back, these examples aren't entirely surprising when looking at Australia's institutional inheritance from Britain. Under the British Empire loyalties were consistently tethered "not to race or ethnicity" but enshrined in a commitment to civic patriotism and Britain's liberal democratic institutions.[12] As the British politician and historian Daniel Hannan explains, the system Australia inherited is built upon critically important principles:

> [l]awmakers should be directly accountable through the ballot box; the executive should be controlled by the legislature; taxes should not be levied, nor laws passed, without popular consent; the individual should be free from arbitrary punishment or

confiscation; decisions should be taken as closely as possible the people they affected; power should be dispersed; no one, not even the head of state, should be above the law; property rights should be secure; disputes should be arbitrated by independent magistrates; freedom of speech, religion, and assembly should be guaranteed.[13]

These are no small ideals. And while Australia can directly trace its institutional lineage to Britain, it's worth recalling that British institutions *themselves* rest upon much deeper historical and philosophical elements, which flow much further back than the writings of Blackstone or the Glorious Revolution.

Greek and Roman ideas of the citizen and the law helped to inform Britain's legal system and institutions. Ancient Greeks, in particular, developed very early ideas of citizenship, democracy and liberty, which combined with innovative thinking on science, rationalism, and philosophy. Later the Romans emphasised systematising the law and defining private property. Even Winston Churchill acknowledged – 'we owe London to Rome'.

Today most Australians, however, are not looking to Rome. We look to Britain. "In pinpointing what makes us distinctively Australian," said Bob Hawke in 1988, "we acknowledge the enormous debt we owe to Britain. Britain has given us the basis of many of the institutions of our free society: our system of Parliamentary democracy, the principles of rule by law and the protection of the rights of the individual under the law, our system of liberal education".[14]

Hawke's point is entirely accurate. In Australia it's not just the 'rule of law' but our other less formal institutions – the way we talk socially about politics and politicians – where we detect an ongoing egalitarianism. An Australian politician, for example, remains unusually accessible and close to the community when compared to officials in many other democracies. Indeed, a Prime Minister like Hawke – with a world record for downing a yard glass of beer (as a Rhodes Scholar, no less) – gained a positive mix of applause and affinity in his time.

But in more serious terms we have a habit of cutting our politicians down to size, which is separate to a lack of trust in politicians. 'Politicians aren't fashionable in Australia,' said Julia Gillard when stepping down as Prime Minister in 2013. Certainly, an Australian legislator has an extremely important and decisive role in society. Yet politicians and even federal ministers don't occupy elite or regal status.

Perhaps the clearest reason behind this is the absence of a House of Lords, which historically never caught on in Australia. The idea of an appointed upper house was passionately and successfully scuttled by early legislators like Daniel Deniehy – one of Australia's earliest republicans. Deniehy, in 1853 coining the term 'bunyip aristocracy', bemoaned "native aristocrats" like William Charles Wentworth and John McArthur, arguing that "the only basis upon which government could be placed" was "the purity of elective principle".[15] Deniehy's desire was for "the inalienable freedom of every colonist upon which to work out the whole organisation and body of our political institution," paving the way for the ballot box to remain the rudder for Australian progress and not simply the province of those with money or political connections.

Australia's voting system, in fact, possesses another distinction to other liberal democracies in that voting has been compulsory since 1924 – a feature that surprises many visitors and overseas observers. The basis for compulsory voting, the Australian political scientist Ian McAllister explains, is "the strong undercurrent of egalitarianism which sees the system as being the fairest means of arriving at a legitimate election outcome".[16] Interestingly, even if compulsory voting were to end, it's predicted that a strong majority of Australians would actually continue to vote.

Voting being open to *all* – at least by federation – was also a key feature of Australian democracy. "In 1901 it was a world first," explains Australian constitutional scholar Helen Irving.[17] "In no other nation were both Houses of Parliament directly elected (even in the United States, senators were appointed up until 1913)," she adds. "The popular referendum for Constitutional alteration (section 128) was employed in only one other country, Switzerland. In addition to the 1902 Commonwealth Act which enfranchised Australian women, and many innovations in electoral procedure, all of this made Australia the most advanced democracy in the world for its time".

Political and legal observations are one thing. But as a non-lawyer I've always found observations of *people* critically more appealing. From egalitarianism flows a natural pragmatism, which also has roots in Australia's early days. A stark need for judgement, sharp decisions and an "iron capacity to carry them out" were essential at a time when wits and endurance met tough reality.[18]

In this environment, the atmosphere was set for 'doing' rather than 'talking'. As the Australian journalist Nick Cater observes, our history shows "a pioneering imperative that rewarded doers rather than thinkers, practical men who fix the fence as opposed to those who deliver papers on agricultural enclosures".[19] It's a sharp point, and very different to a modern economy where, physically, much less gets built and much more gets administered. In early Australia, an attachment to ideology, or extended hypothesising, offered little when practical matters were priority.

Boom Time – 1850s Onward

From at least 1850 onward Australia changed considerably. Settlers, for one, were farming more and more land. From 1850 to 1900, the area of land used to cultivate wheat alone expanded twenty times over.[20]

More colonists meant, inevitably, the opportunity for more clashes, but also more positive interactions, with the continent's expansive and highly diverse Indigenous population – a point I'll return to later.

With the discovery of gold in Victoria and New South Wales, Australia's population doubled from 1850 to 1860. From the 1850s onward, Australia began the process of building an enterprising but more cosmopolitan and savvy population.

At around this time Samuel Smiles' book *Self Help* had sold a respectable 20,000 copies in England. This motivational piece threaded neatly with popular enlightenment thinking of self-improvement, and was a readable thrust towards "stimulating men to elevate and improve themselves by their own free and independent individual action".[21] Critical of "individual idleness, selfishness and vice", it prompted hard but smart work among individuals as the vehicle for social and economic progress. "With a trowel in his hand and a book in his pocket," Smiles also encouraged self-education for the working man. Although for an English audience, *Self Help* was a symbolic but real-world template for the soon-to-be nation of Australia, where not only British settlers but Pacific Islanders, Americans, Chinese, West Indians, and others were now scratching towards a brighter future.

By 1881 nearly half of Australia's 2.3 million population had been born outside Australia – another point I'll return to later. Many brought with them not only energy but, according to Thomas Barlow, "foreign know-how and strong connections to the outside world".[22]

Thoroughly modern patriot

The innovations following the gold rush took obvious pressure off back-breaking work. Toward the end of the 1800s, Australia became a standout example of where the demand for raw materials, with innovation and an enterprising frontier spirit, generates growth and prosperity. "Our prospects are better here than at home," declared the fictional young American hero – Harry – from Horatio Alger's 1893 *In a New World*. Alger's rags-to-riches tales were immensely popular at the time, reflecting the benefits of capitalism, and the value of respectability overlapping with reward. Australia, as measured by consumption and wealth per head, was *the* wealthiest nation in the world leading up to federation.

There's a natural tendency to believe that, in the churn of economic dynamism, unvarnished selfishness would emerge as a defining social theme. Today, especially, economic success can be code for excessive individualism. But it appears that ideas of mutuality and collective responsibility actually re-energised in the late 1800s and, even for those in rough circumstances, a healthy regard for 'community' endured. Miles Franklin's 1901 classic *My Brilliant Career* captures some of the 'social capital' and mutual trust in Australia at this time. Here is Franklin, for example, writing about her family's items being repossessed while in Goulburn, New South Wales:

> But for the generosity of our relatives we would have been in a pretty plight. They sent us sufficient means to buy everything, and our neighbours came to our rescue with enthusiasm and warm-hearted

> genuine sympathy. The bailiff – a gentleman to the core – seeing how matters stood, helped us to the utmost of his power.[23]

Other examples show that Australians were thinking not only of each other but beyond the provincial confines of direct neighbours, and various states and towns. During the 1870s Indian famine, for example, the predecessor of the Australian Football League gave its entire gate takings to famine relief efforts. This may seem inconsequential now but, back then, it symbolised unique sympathy and charity on a global scale. Over a century later we'd see similar efforts for the 2004 Boxing Day Tsunami. Although the 1870s famine relief effort aided another colony of the Empire, it serves as a perfect application of the Australian poet Adam Lindsay Gordon's words, 'Kindness in another's trouble, courage in your own'.

In 1868, in building on the themes of sport and social cohesion, the first Australian sporting team travelled overseas. This was a major achievement in itself. But it is more eye-opening in that it was actually an Aboriginal XI – what we'd now call an Indigenous All Stars Team. Playing a decent forty-seven cricket matches throughout England over seven months, records show they won fourteen matches, lost fourteen, and drew nineteen.

It's not too surprising that, from not just national sports teams but growing feelings of solidarity, ideas of nationalism and federation began to emerge. In the absence of social media, poetry was the medium for federal expression, and the steam engine and telegraph meant more people connecting across the continent. *The Dominion of Australia: A Forecast*, written by school headmaster James Brunton Stephens in 1878, is credited as one of the first 'federation poems'. In many poems to come, a sense of fraternalism was reinforced over anti-federation forces of "selfishness, greed, and faction".[24] Clearly many soon-to-be Australians, from across the continent, were starting to feel part of something bigger.

Founding Fathers

Linking this national sentiment together required another type of national asset – good leadership. In a nation where a name like Ned Kelly tends to ring more bells than Barton, Parkes or Reid, it's not surprising that many Australians know little of their own unique founding fathers.[25] Key leaders from over a century ago, these men now seem distant strangers. But their actions were essential in pulling together the political foundation of modern Australia.

Although viewed as a mere formality, federating the colonies was tough work. Like any sizeable and well thought out reform, federation required extensive consultation to find sufficient 'conciliation, conference, and common sense' among the colonies.[26] From defence to trade, differing and competing views – some hard headed, some dreamers – emerged at various Constitutional Conventions throughout the 1890s. But there were also key differences between the men shaping federation.

Henry Parkes – Australia's 'Father of Federation' – had scraped his way up from humble beginnings in England to high political office in Australia. Forced off the family farm in Warwickshire because of his father's debt when eight years old, Parkes was a man who knew hardship from early on. With a confessed "very limited and imperfect" formal education, he arrived in Sydney and found employment as a labourer, then went into iron-mongering and brass-foundry.[27] In the early 1850s, failing at various business ventures he eventually waded into the threes Ps – publishing, politics and poetry – eventually sparking a career as a stirring advocate of federation and five-time Premier of New South Wales. "Instead of a confusion of names and geographical divisions, which so perplexes many people at a distance," Parkes famously said when envisioning a new nation, "we shall be Australians, and a people with 7,000 miles of coast, more than 2,000,000 square miles of land, with 4,000,000 of population, and shall present ourselves to the world as 'Australia'".[28] Parkes, however, died in 1896 before formal federation was achieved.

By contrast, a younger George Reid came from more privileged settings. He was a man, however, who overcame his own less obvious personal hurdles. Sporting a decent education but a "lazy horror of Greek".[29] Reid showed talent with numbers and technical detail, which steered him toward an early stint in the New South Wales Treasury and, later, as Secretary of the Attorney-General's Department. He brought to government a coherent liberal philosophy across matters

Thoroughly modern patriot

of trade, local government and public finance, which he applied when becoming Governor of New South Wales in the early 1890s. His policies, with their 'free trade' design, gnawed at the protectionism of the times. A sturdy philosophy supplemented by awesome oratory is potent in politics. And Reid supposedly "topped the poll" as the best platform speaker in the British Empire – certainly no easy accolade.[30]

Free trade was a central passion to Reid. But he was also a renowned pragmatist. As late as 1898 he famously reneged on a vote for the draft national Constitution that he actually helped write. Determining there were problems with the draft, Reid discouraged many New South Welshmen from voting in favour (even though he would vote for it himself). Dare a politician change his mind, this earned him a 'fence-sitter' reputation as 'yes-no Reid'. Without Reid's influence, however, the trajectory of federation could've been much different. He was Australia's fourth prime minister, serving from 1904 to 1905.

Edmund Barton, like Reid, emerged from rather privileged circumstances. Yet with a father who had gone broke more than once Barton and his eight siblings knew tough circumstances. As Australia's first Prime Minister, Barton could be said to be 'famously-not-famous' among Australian schoolchildren, and adults, for being mistaken as American President George Washington.

Despite his achievements Barton is a figure that appeared to have no superb characteristics. In his early years, for example, Reid (then a good friend) said he was a "deficient speaker" despite emerging later as an articulate performer – something that, like all of us, can be developed with practice. Reading Barton's professional career shows a man facing many political losses, constantly coming in second or third when votes were cast or key positions emerged. But according to Barton's biographer, the late Geoffrey Bolton, Barton possessed, like the greats John Monash and John Curtin, a "peculiar capacity to lift in moments of crisis and so to make a lasting contribution to public welfare".[31]

Despite their differences, Australia's unofficial fathers of federation shared two broad similarities. The first was a keen and obvious affection for country. Australian politics at this time offered little remuneration and a political career, arguably, carried a sharpened attachment to public service. Until quite recently, in fact, national politicians maintained private initiatives to supplement their parliamentary incomes. Even Robert Menzies – Australia's longest serving Prime Minister – at times took up part time legal work to support his parliamentary income.

Second, we find in these leaders 'real world' experience so essential for public life. The Athenian experience of 'what is sweet in life and what is terrible' grounded but also guided many of Australia's political leaders in the early years of federation. One can find in their characters lessons of persistence, heartbreak, aspiration and improvement, which in this case certainly went beyond income or one's start in life.

Thoroughly modern patriot

It's worth mentioning here that political leadership in Australia did, of course, not start in 1901 or in the lead up to federation. Australia's early British governors – extensively well-accomplished and well-travelled – were also driven by a unique sense of service, discipline and wise practical experience.

Arthur Phillip, for example, fought in the Seven Years War in Cuba before seconding to the Portuguese Navy prior to taking on the unwanted mission of Australian settlement. Lachlan Macquarie – immortalised in the names of various Sydney institutions – shared a breadth of experience with service in North America, Jamaica, India and Egypt. Shades of such cosmopolitan experience were applied in the new colony under the leadership of various governors. Through his 'enlightened despotism', for example, Macquarie designed policies to improve social conditions by stimulating pastoral activity, building infrastructure and helping to secure the employment prospects of emancipists. Bligh, who had also served across the globe, possessed a similar understanding of people but a seemingly consistent penchant to apply the rules. Despite being at the centre of Australia's first and (so far) only coup, Bligh's persistence reined in excessive military trading and manipulation. It could be argued that without Bligh's doggedness for order the colony could've diverged onto a very different path.

So, What Does This All Mean?

All of these issues – threadbare beginnings, upward growth and mobility for convicts, our social egalitarianism, and sound leadership – show that we've evolved considerably since, and even well before, federation.

The royal commission that not only sent Cook but Phillip our way, the Governors that shaped the early colonies, the evolving British rule of law and institutional scaffolding, and our selection of a constitutional monarchy at federation, all point to the importance of the Crown to Australia's legal and social development.

It would be a mistake to move away from these foundational and ongoing elements of success. But not all share this concern.

3

Too Broad A Church: What's Driving An Aussie Republic?

Australian republicans, as the general saying goes, are a broad church. Their motivations, similar to monarchists, are expansive. But unlike monarchists, their modern goals can appear so varied that they seem contradictory.

Some are unhappy with the British Monarchy, animated by opposition to hereditary privilege, while others regret that our so-called 'Head of State' can have the power to dismiss a prime minister. Other republicans note the frustration of having to explain to foreign guests *why* the Queen's portrait hangs on the wall of government offices and our foreign embassies. Perception in Asia is also a significant driver of republican concerns, especially the need to offset the confusion of near neighbours in securing trade and commercial transactions.

Even *sustainability* has featured in the republican cause. In 1999, in the lead up to the centenary of federation, one leading republican figure said the movement was "to bring about a fair, just, and environmentally sustainable republic".[1] A 'reconciled republic' – meaning the formal relationship with Indigenous Australia – has added mixed goals to the republican cause.

Republican Impulses

These modern objectives are slightly at odds to the republican goals of previous generations. In the 1850s, prior to federation, Australian republicans tethered themselves mainly to self-governing democratic ideals and independence from Britain, which were closely tied to land reform and an end to convict transportation.

At the time, these were understandable aspirations. Convict labour in the Australian colony was reaching the end of its life, with the franchise – meaning the right to vote – tightly held by property owners. For over half a century, republican ideals – the Battle of Concord's 1775 'shot heard round the world' – were transmitting from the United States of America with great appeal. When asked if America were to be a 'monarchy or a republic', it was the great Benjamin Franklin's immortal reply – 'a republic, ma'am, if you can keep it' – that set the tone of modern aspirational democratic self-government.

Closer to home it was John Dunmore Lang – Presbyterian minister, activist, politician and writer – who emerged as the central figure in the Australian republican movement. Lang's 1852 "*Freedom and Independence for the Golden Lands of Australia* was, and remains, the definitive treatise on Australian republicanism," according to one of Australia's leading republican intellectuals today.[2] In this work Lang marshalled a series of arguments impenetrable to a modern Australian audience. Yet he also appealed to coherent themes of maturity and 'coming of age' – themes that modern republicans, such as Paul Keating, have also appealed to in more recent times. In 1851, Lang told a Sydney audience that New South Wales has an:

> inherent right to entire freedom and independence, whenever it is both able and willing to undertake the management of its own affairs, without either assistance or protection from the parent state: just as a son, when he comes of age, and creates a business and forms a household of his own, is thenceforth legally free from all parental control.[3]

Interestingly, Henry Parkes ran in the same circles as Lang, at least in Parkes' younger years. Parkes, however, distanced himself when it came to colonial autonomy and Britain's role, believing future self-government didn't mean completely evolving out of Britain's orbit.

Coming to federation what we learn, and what all Australians know, is that our independence experience was entirely benign. Australians clearly weren't upset with the English Crown in the same way as, say, Americans. Fighting no revolutionary wars, it was the steady work of impatient patriots – some republican, some monarchist, some country folk, some city folk – that combined in shaping Australian federation. As even the late Australian historian John Hirst – a devoted republican – observed, "Republicanism was not needed in order to achieve control over local affairs and democracy too was established without a disowning of Britain".[4]

In turn, no serious republican claims seemed to surface in the post-federation era. Indeed, it seems most criticisms of Australia's British connections of this time, and right up until World War Two, have tended to be retrospective. If one reads Malcolm Turnbull's 1993 *The Reluctant Republic*, for example, a noticeable portion is spent criticising Australia's excessively practical Constitution, the influence of British figures like Lord Curzon on Australia's early foreign policy, and what Turnbull labels Australia's "docile obedience to British wishes throughout the first half of the century".[5] Turnbull also cites a common target in Britain's strategic conduct during World War Two – the failure to provide air support to defend Singapore.

Not all, however, is retrospective. In the post-war era, questions of identity and 'thinking big' began to quietly emerge. Geoffrey Dutton's 1963 edited collection of essays – *Australia and the Monarchy* – is seen as a detectable watermark in the republican cause, with Dutton questioning why Australians shied away from "self-knowledge, from asking ourselves who we really are, from answering why the head of state is not Australian".[6] Alongside the 1975 dismissal of Gough Whitlam, this added a renewed emphasis to an otherwise slumbering discussion.

The Dismissal

Whitlam had come to power in 1972, appealing to fresh themes of change and, as some Australians will recall, 'It's time'. A politician enthusiastic about the role of government, Whitlam increased the size of the federal budget, made an unprecedented range of commitments, and, in just three years, delivered a new national anthem, created a new non-British honours system and abolished national service.

The Governor-General Sir John Kerr's dismissal of Whitlam – a point I'll unpack further below – antagonised Australians unenthused about Britain's links to Australia. It also highlighted, for republicans, Palace overreach and the legitimacy of 'reserve powers'.

A Focus On The Governor-General

Indeed, these events tapped *the* focal points of Australia's modern republican cause – the role and powers of the Governor-General. The range of republican models imply subtle but important differences – direct election, parliamentary approval or appointment. But it is the role of the Governor-General that corrals their modern focus and concern. Here is Turnbull, writing again in *The Reluctant Republic*:

> I believe, as do my colleagues in the Australian Republican Movement, that an Australian President should have the same powers and functions as the Governor-General currently exercises. Those

powers, as we have seen, are defined by both the terms of the Constitution and the Constitutional conventions. The President should be a Head of State but not a Head of Government. The real political power should remain with the Prime Minister.[7]

It should be noted this isn't simply replacing the position title from Governor-General to 'President' – what came to be known as the 'tippex option'. Republicans propose changes to significant portions of our Constitution – removing references to the Queen, codifying specific powers on dissolution, creating a new oath, establishing a more acute role for the High Court, and stipulating where the President is permitted to source their legal advice. Not to mention the method of appointing the President – a contestable debate in itself among republicans. Lines of the Constitution, literally, would be taken out with new pages added.

Amid this new set of Constitutional rules republican lobbyists also add a strong coat of provincialism. An Australian President, according to Turnbull, should be someone "who lives among us, breathes the air we breathe, hurts when we hurt, cheers when we win, encourages us when we lose and always barracks for Australia".[8]

Hereditary Privilege

It is here where we locate the other chief driver of modern Australian republicanism – a hostility to Buckingham Palace. But, even more specifically than this, it is hereditary privilege that truly has the capacity to agitate many republicans. "Could anyone on this side of the Enlightenment walk through a maternity ward," asks one Australian republican intellect, "and make a rational argument that one baby is inherently superior to all others?"[9]

Challenging 'inherent superiority' also mixes with common democratic terms like transparency, openness and elections – terms that most Australians appreciate but are slightly misplaced when discussing how a constitutional monarchy actually functions and the role of the Governor-General. As the Australian Republic Movement notes, "It's not right for Australia's democracy to be subject to a foreign monarch," but it's also "wrong that Australians cannot become our head of state and that we have no say in who does".[10]

The British monarchy has also been accused by republican lobbyists of representing sectarianism, vested interests and privilege. Even sexism is linked to the monarchy in some arguments. Republicans further pounce on any royal inconsistency – a move that appears largely more tactical than philosophical – questioning whether Prince Andrew, for example, is fit enough to be Australia's 'eighth in line' to Australia's head of state. The Palace Letters saga, where republican lobbyists hoped to implicate the Queen in Whitlam's dismissal, provide a further example.

4

A Monarchist's Response

In untangling these modern and historical republican drivers, it's clear a significant amount has changed since the 1999 referendum. The centennial urgency of the 'republican moment' has passed – it's less important, for example, who should be opening the Sydney 2000 Olympics, and we seem increasingly less concerned with the Governor-General representing Australia overseas. We've also seen year on year trade and commercial relations only *improve* with Asia – trends that monarchists and other 'no' voters in 1999 were told would recede.

Indeed, in not just the past twenty years, but throughout the twentieth century, pragmatic winds have steadily blown through republican sales. God Save the Queen is no longer Australia's national anthem, we now have our own honours system and the oath for new citizens no longer mentions the Queen. Buckingham Palace has also made more than clear that, when it comes to controversial political problems, as in November 1975, it is the Governor-General and not the Queen that takes decisive action. Clearly, Australians do not think of themselves as British like we did, say, before the 1950s.

And neither do foreigners. A great example of this – a favourite of mine – is from a 1942 cultural training booklet given to wartime American Servicemen deployed to Australia. "A member of the British Commonwealth, Australia is a British dominion, a member of the British Commonwealth of Nations – but that doesn't mean Britain owns or rules Australia," the pocketbook reads.[1] "The Australians govern themselves, as a separate nation, sending their own diplomatic representatives overseas and managing their own relations with foreign nations. At the same time, there are certain traditional ties with Great Britain which the Australians value". It perfectly captures the organic balance we've found – as far back as the 1940s – between heritage and 'coming of age'.

I sense that, if an 1850s John Dunmore Lang looked at Australia today, he'd be – if not slightly pleased – satisfied to the point of applying his republican energy to other progressive reforms. Yet modern republican lobbyists appear no Dunmore Langs, unlikely to settle and certainly not eager to redirect their energies. And here we turn to properly understanding the role of their primary focus – the Governor-General.

Understanding The Office

Any look at the office of the Governor-General – at least in modern times – isn't complete without exploring the considered thoughts of late Australian statesman Paul Hasluck. Hasluck, a Governor-General himself from

1969 to 1974, used the 1979 Queale Memorial Lecture to sketch *how* the office works within our unique system of constitutional monarchy, parliamentary democracy and federation.[2] Importantly, he captured some of the localised intricacies of the office that had developed over half a century.

Strictly speaking "the Governor-General is the direct representative in Australia of Her Majesty the Queen," writes Hasluck. They are "not the representative of the Queen of England," he adds, but the "representative of the Queen of Australia". Granted, when monarchists speak like this, things can be slightly confusing. But the Queen and the Governor-General's roles are clarified in a number of practical ways that most Australians understand.

First, the Queen is not involved in everyday affairs in Australia. And neither, really, is the Governor-General. "The Governor-General is not placed in a position where he can run the Parliament, run the Courts or run any of the instrumentalities of government," explains Hasluck, "but he occupies a position where he can help ensure that those who conduct the affairs of the nation do so strictly in accordance with the Constitution and the laws of the Commonwealth and with due regard to the public interest". Thus the Governor-General plays the role of a 'neutral umpire', or the train conductor 'above politics' – officiating visits, opening parliament, signing bills into law and, in the case of parliamentary deadlock, convening joint sittings to drive resolution.

Thoroughly modern patriot

The second practicality many Australians understand is that the position of Governor-General is now filled by Australians, and no longer handpicked by Buckingham Palace or British officials. Well before Governors-General like Quentin Bryce or Peter Cosgrove the office was largely held by earls, viscounts and barons – a practice unthinkable today.

If we go back to the First Fleet – 1788 – the position of governor was held by a string of distinguished and highly-cosmopolitan naval men who were more well-travelled than most Australians today. Toward the end of the nineteenth century the position was expected to support itself. Therefore, according to the late Victorian Governor and republican Richard McGarvie, "Aristocracy and affluence became necessary conditions of office".[3]

State Governors, too, offer an even more diverse picture of Australians, with examples such as the iconic Indigenous Australian Sir Douglas Nicholls in South Australia (serving from 1976-1977) or the current Governor Hieu Van Le – a former South Vietnamese refugee.

The third practicality is that Australian governors-general have added unique character to the office. As the social scientist Donald Markwell notes, each have brought their own emphasis to the role, depending largely on the currents and crises of the time:

> the 'touch of healing' of Sir Zelman Cowen (1977–

82), the further calming and dignified energy of Sir Ninian Stephen (1982–89), the initially controversial but then largely quiet years of Mr Bill Hayden (1989–96), the energetic — some say too energetic — focus of Sir William Deane on Indigenous issues and reconciliation and the clever symbolism of the Deane years (1996–2001), the controversy that unfairly engulfed Dr Peter Hollingworth (2001–03), the stabilisation and energetic if unobtrusive conscientiousness of Major General Michael Jeffrey (2003–08), and the vibrant inclusiveness of Dame Quentin Bryce (2008–14).[4]

All of these elements – the localised emphasis of the office to Australia, the steady changes, the slow but measured untethering from Britain – underscore that the Governor-General has not stayed 'stuck in time' but kept pace with events and expectations. "An Australian Governor-General, representing and acting on behalf of the Australian head of state, the Queen," notes Hasluck, "is not the same as an Australian Governor-General performing his functions in the early days of Federation". As he further explains:

> In 1901, even the status of Dominion was unknown. Today we have grown into a stage of independence and international recognition that was never envisaged in 1901. The Queen herself is now Queen of Australia and in matters concerning Australia acts solely on the advice of her Australian Ministers. Australia in her own right and identity as a nation appoints and receives Ambassadors. Her treaty-

making power is exercised freely. Australia goes to war by her own decision and makes other decisions in her relations with foreign countries independently of any decisions made or not made on the same subjects by other members of the Commonwealth of Nations. What an Australian Government might advise our head of state to do on many subjects is in some cases quite different from what some other government in the Commonwealth of Nations might advise the Queen to do. We have international interests today which were not known in 1901.[5]

The Use Of Reserve Powers

Many republicans won't deny some of these modernising factors. But what about the reserve powers – the power, essentially, to dismiss a prime minister? For Hasluck, the example of the 1975 dismissal wasn't an issue of whether this power was permissible 'or not' but *facts* justifying the *use* of the power itself.

So what were the facts? By November 1975 Whitlam couldn't pass supply – what Americans call 'a government shutdown'. His attempts to borrow funds outside the Australian Treasury through dubious intermediaries clearly showed poor judgement. And it violated opposition leader Malcolm Fraser's principle to keep the government on life support if it could avoid 'reprehensible and extraordinary events'.

Whitlam did not want to step down. Or call a full election,

which clearly left Kerr in an impossible position. Acting within the powers of the office, he steered to where democracies need to go in such times of uncertainty – the people. "Within a few weeks," noted John Howard, "the Australian people could decide whether or not they agreed or disagreed with Mr Whitlam or Mr Fraser".[6] They strongly disagreed with Whitlam.

At a time of political logjam, especially when one looks to the world's leading republic – the United States – one can't help think of the appeal and efficiency of our government shutdown resolution mechanism. America has had 21 shutdowns since 1976. We've had only one. Decisiveness and authority clearly aren't the only criteria for powers around a head of state. But they sure come close.

Looking back on the dismissal I sense, as a fair-minded monarchist, we can learn three things. First, and rather obviously, it was a wrenching episode in Australian political history. I don't say this lightly – we never want to repeat a prime minister being dismissed by a Governor-General.

Second, I sense most Australians appreciate that it was a series of serious Whitlam missteps, rather than any Palace manipulation, that ultimately led to Whitlam's sacking. Subsequent to the excessively highlighted 'Palace Letters' affair, we've since learned that the Queen played no part, other than being apprised of events.

And third, do we need to codify reserve powers, as

republicans are so eager to do? Indeed, this is *the* fundamental question of the republic debate in our time. My position is simply this – rather than adding pages of rules in the Australian Constitution, future situations where reserve powers – or any powers requiring the Governor-General's acute discretion – tend to be more an 'art' than a science. This is entirely Hasluck's timeless point about the facts justifying the means – not the other way around.

Of the dismissal much is still made, for example, over Kerr speaking to the Chief Justice of the High Court – Anthony Mason – in seeking advice on potential solutions. Some have seriously suggested that Kerr should've taken advice from the Attorney-General – a minister in Whitlam's government – or, in recent times, that the Solicitor-General be the binding 'go to' for legal advice.

So who should be the *right* source of legal advice for the Governor-General? The answer is a mix. In defence of Kerr, and any future Governor-General, a Chief High Court justice is *exactly* the kind of person I'd expect the office to confer with in making seismic decisions on responsible government. Or, at times, it might mean the Attorney-General – as it already is at times on some procedural matters. In other situations, it may be the Solicitor-General – as was the case when Quentin Bryce sought advice on appointing Rudd as Prime Minister (after Gillard's departure).

Latitude and discretion, after all, are key. Especially

on issues that none of us can accurately predict. It is very difficult to see where constraining the powers of the Governor-General would result in the office bringing swift resolution to any future political crises.

Hereditary Privilege, Political Evolution

Over the years I've been asked to feature on radio to respond to various monarchist issues. It's certainly not a full-time job. But Prince Harry's 2020 secession from his royal responsibilities caused an unusually high spike in royal interest.

Was this, I was constantly asked, a sign of monarchical decline? And how was the monarchy still relevant to Australia? The best answer I could offer at the time, and still can, is that the British monarchy is a *modern* monarchy in *modern* times.

Even just tracking the Queen herself – over a half century – illustrates impressive themes of 'growth' and 'evolution'. In 1953, when taking the throne at just 25, world figures included Churchill, Stalin and Eisenhower. Now it is BoJo, Putin and Biden. In 1949, just eight nations created the Commonwealth. Today membership comprises 53 states and 2.4 billion people.

The ascension itself – marked by the twin pressures of intense grief and responsibility – has required an obvious steadfastness in the face of ever-present challenge. Three decades of troubles in Northern Ireland, jarred by bombings and guerrilla warfare, was further laced with symbolic personal attacks and threat. And 1992 – labelled 'Annus horribilis' – saw divorces and separation, the death of a nephew, new levels of media intrusion and a fire at Windsor Castle. More recent times have also been 'active' in royal terms – the Westminster logjam around Brexit, Prince Andrew's associations, Phillip's death and the frenzied commentary around the Duke and Duchess of Sussex.

These moments represent a seismic departure from a time when intrigue, scandals, divorce and family openness were much more taboo. But they expose the human pressures that require personal and public leadership – something that, royal or not, we can all share. The Crown appeals because it has stayed largely relevant to modern societal expectations. Indeed, the Queen has lived her Golden Jubilee declaration that managing constant change 'has become an expanding discipline' and that 'the way we embrace it defines our future'.

In terms of social touchpoints with Australia, the royal relationship has also clearly changed. Upon the Queen's visit to Australia in 1954, when asked to a local ball, her majesty did not "attend balls given by commoners", notes the Australian historian Jim Davidson.[7] But, by 1977, Prince Charles was appearing on television shows with colourful Australian TV presenter Molly Meldrum, promoting the Queen's Jubilee Appeal in between Meldrum's "yeahs and ums".[8]

Back in Britain, the Palace's response to family change

reveals even more of a pivot to modern expectations. As Davidson concedes:

> Consider how far already the Queen has adapted: from forbidding her sister Margaret marrying a divorced man, in 1955, to giving her blessing to the wedding of Wills and Kate – who had been 'practising as a couple', as Prince Charles put it, for eight years. Kate Middleton is the first commoner to marry someone directly in line to the throne, or a king, since the time of Henry VIII.[9]

Observations on royal evolution are important. But it's also key to look at the institutions that underpin the monarchy and how these, in themselves, have far from remained stuck in time. "The story of how the English Monarch changed from national leader (and sometimes oppressor) into international symbol (and guardian of freedom)," wrote Tony Abbott in his 1995 book *The Minimal Monarchy*, "is one of the great political evolutions in Western history".[10]

A full-blown account of British history between the eleventh and seventeenth centuries is beyond the scope of these pages. Except to just make three brief points.

First, a move away from total monarchy has been a titanic struggle over centuries. "In establishing the rule of law," recently quipped former British Prime Minister Gordon Brown, "the first five centuries are always the hardest".[11] Brown's point is a good one. There were at least nine major civil wars during the period from the Norman Conquest to the Glorious Revolution.

Second, the motivating factors for these struggles have generally centred on two things – legitimacy and taxation. From King Henry II (late 1100s), and after the first iteration of the Magna Carta (1215), a steady precedent was established to summon councils to seek 'advice' and discuss levies. If the King did not do this, he risked de-legitimising himself and his endeavours, which generally involved foreign wars and keeping domestic order. These councils grew into what we now know as parliament which, in itself, has taken hundreds of years to evolve into anything resembling what we know today.

Third, parliamentarians have also over-extended the gradual compromise between the throne and parliament. British parliamentarians captured and executed Charles I in 1649. But in 1660, a new parliament voted to restore the monarchy, with Charles II called out of exile and crowned in 1661.[12]

It's important to be absolutely clear here – outrunning total monarchy has been an overwhelmingly positive development in the history of democracy. This is especially the case for Australia, considering how *different* our democracy would have turned out had the First Fleet landed a century earlier (or landed at all).

Both the Queen's story, and the historical political evolution of the monarchy, commends itself to many as a picture of growth and legitimacy. Labelling them as prisoners to vested interests, or privilege, isn't likely to win many arguments among Australians. Indeed, how the Crown has continued to find footing and appeal offers a great story. Especially in places where we least suspect.

5

Indigenous Australians And The Monarchy's Promise

At the 1998 Constitutional Convention, despite the scores of eminent Australians in attendance, far and away the most notable speech was by Neville Bonner. Bonner had risen from inauspicious beginnings – literally born under a tree in northern New South Wales – to become a federal senator for Queensland. He was a very proud Indigenous man but, in a manner that confronts assumptions, was conservative in his politics, disposition and philosophy. This put him in lonely company, especially given the activism of the 1960s and 1970s – the era of Bonner's political awakening and ascent.

By the 1998 Convention he had been out of representative politics for nearly two decades. Reading slowly from prepared notes, and at times losing his place, he scolded the Convention for considering a disposal of the Crown:

> You told my people that your system was best. We have come to accept that ... The dispossessed, despised adapted to your system. Now you say that you were wrong and that we were wrong to believe

you ... What is most hurtful is that after all we have learned together, after subjugating us and then freeing us, once again you are telling us that you know better. How dare you? How dare you?[1]

Bonner died the following year. But his observation endures – an outrage that, after years of striving towards "the system", the goalposts were being moved just that little bit further away. Indeed, Bonner pounced on the embarrassment and uncertainty of the republican objective. What precisely were Indigenous Australians – indeed all Australians – to gain from it?

In a notable contrast, Bonner's first embrace after his speech was with the late Indigenous leader Gatjil Djerrkura, who was then the chair of the since-disbanded Aboriginal and Torres Strait Islander Commission. Djerrkura did not share Bonner's attachment to the Crown. Like many others, Djerrkura saw the republican objective as an opportunity for reconciliation but was less captured by typical republican impulses – our image in Asia, for example, or an untethering from Britain. "A republic that does not make the first concrete gesture towards reconciliation is a republic that walks in the footsteps of the Crown," he said. "Is this the impoverished vision of a republic we want? My answer is 'No'. Our vision must be more substantial ... My dream is of Australia as a reconciled republic".[2]

But a 'reconciled republic', however, forms only part of a wider commitment for Indigenous recognition. This has been a much longer journey than calls for a republic

– from William Cooper's 1937 letter to King George VI and the 1963 Yirrkala Bark Petitions, to Julia Gillard's 2010 Expert Panel and the more recent Referendum Council commissioned by Malcolm Turnbull and Bill Shorten. Understandably, a republic offers a great deal to advocates of reconciliation – a chance to renovate our foundational system of government and, in doing so, seek even further recognition for Indigenous Australians. But when push comes to shove, according to lawyer Noel Pearson, "It would be grossly unfair if the Indigenous recognition referendum is not first cab off the rank for a referendum".[3]

While for many the focus is clear – Constitutional recognition – the outcomes have become opaque. The mandate for the Referendum Council under Prime Minister Turnbull, for example, was to consult the public and report on options for a referendum proposal. Yet what was offered in return was a vague concept for a national indigenous assembly – vastly different from public expectations of wording for a preamble or a blueprint on changes to Constitutional text. This assembly, as Prime Minister Turnbull noted, would essentially be a third chamber of parliament, inconsistent with equal civic rights and the existing structure of the Senate and House of Representatives. He said the government did "not believe such a radical change to our Constitution's representative institutions has any realistic prospect of being supported by a majority of Australians in a majority of States".[4] In my view he was right.

Thoroughly modern patriot

The devil for Indigenous Constitutional recognition, like the republican movement, is in the detail. And, like Bonner's criticism of a republic, it is difficult to see how recognition would actually help Indigenous Australians prosper in a modern world. "If Australia became a republic," said Bonner, "we, the Aboriginal people, would be no better off because the changes that are needed to help us don't include republican status. I see no point".[5]

Bonner's support for the Crown, like his politics, confronted assumptions. And there are few better explanations for this than that given by Tony Abbott in the 2010 Neville Bonner Oration:

> To Bonner, the Crown represented what was best in English-speaking civilisation. It was the British government that had commanded the settlers to live in amity with the native people. It was Governor Phillip who had refused to take punitive action against the Aborigines who speared him. It was the Crown courts, uncowed by local public opinion, that had sentenced white men to hang for the murder of black people. The actual treatment of black people might often have mocked notions of equality before the law. Discrimination in so many aspects of daily life might have betrayed the noble ideal of the brotherhood of man. Still, the system was supposed to guarantee to everyone the ancient rights and freedoms of Englishmen and sometimes it actually did. Unlike those who saw enough of its failings to reject it, he saw enough of its strengths to

embrace it. After all, it was the Crown that could be appealed to for justice. Some of the Crown's agents were often harsh, even brutal, but for much of our settled existence, they were the only protection that Aborigines had from the tyranny of the mob.

From the moment the First Fleet landed, Governor Phillip sought to make peace with Indigenous Australians. In fact, he carried specific instructions from King George III to "endeavour by every possible means to open an intercourse with the natives, and to conciliate their affections, enjoining all our subjects to live in amity and kindness with them".[6]

Granted, with an ever-expanding frontier, conciliation was not always how things turned out. As settlers pushed across the continent, displacement occurred among Indigenous Australians while, at the same time, law and order could not always keep up. It was not just settlements and farms being established but entirely new colonies: Western Australia in 1829, South Australia in 1834, Victoria in 1851 and Queensland in 1859. As the Referendum Council reported, in a summary of the waves of Indigenous history, "it is a story of triumph and failure, pride and regret, celebration and sorrow, greatness and shame".[7]

Yet as Abbott suggests, and as Bonner believed, from our earliest days our British Constitutional inheritance strove to do the best it could. The reality, as David Kemp writes in *The Land of Dreams*, "was that the instruments of law enforcement available were too weak to impose the law beyond the settled areas".[8] I believe most Australians look back at those frontier days with a strong dose of common sense – that our system is not flawless but still a great deal better than the non-democratic alternatives of administration that existed at the time. When ultimately weighed, the persuasion and appeal of the protections and opportunities that life offers in mainstream Australia have overwhelmingly delivered more good than harm.

Therefore, assimilation and integration, which used to be 'fighting words' for some, are now the key themes of actual experience for overwhelming numbers of Indigenous Australians. As I wrote in my short biography of Bonner:

> Nearly 70% of people of Aboriginal descent now live in urban areas and stand testament to Bonner's philosophy of self-determination. On the other hand, encouraging Aboriginals to live entirely separate lives from mainstream Australians – an initiative Bonner detested – has had devastating and tragic consequences for Aboriginals in remote areas.[9]

If such integration is a key attribute among Indigenous Australians today, then another more historic element is diversity – a point not always fully acknowledged by activists, government officials and even former prime ministers. Latent in Kevin Rudd's National Apology, for example, or Paul Keating's Redfern Address, is a tendency to collectively address "Aboriginal Australia" without acknowledging the differences and inequalities *within* Aboriginal culture and society. With 700 distinct groups speaking more than 250 languages, professing any uniformity has its obvious hurdles. On the one hand, for instance, one might find legendary exchanges between figures like Bennelong and Governor Phillip but in other instances indifference or outright hostility. "All they seem'd to want," as Captain Cook wrote in his diary, "was for us to be gone".[10] The Southern Cross on the Australian flag, too, may have status with the legend of Mululu of the Kanda tribe, but what about the Jagera or Turrbal?

Contrasts also expose capabilities. In 1846, Tasmanian Aborigines exiled on Flinders Island appealed to Queen Victoria about maltreatment and lack of good faith by colonial authorities. They did so the way most Australians today lobby government—by petition. But how many groups were aware of a petition process, or had the capability to use such mechanisms? Today, as the politics of Constitutional recognition have shown, compressing such diversity and inequality into a single gesture of words is bound to be confronted by challenges.

Yet it is exactly with such diversity where we see the value in not just shared institutions but the Crown itself – a symbol evoking tradition, custom and continuity. Indeed, there is something instructive in this, especially when looking at the Crown's appeal in PNG, where there is even more diversity jammed into less geography. My mother is of the Sui clan of New Ireland Province, for example, yet the clan is one of over a thousand culturally distinct groups throughout not just the archipelagos but the PNG Highlands. As I noted earlier, little homogeneity beyond the family group makes wide consensus difficult and politics atomising. By contrast, the idea of the Crown commands a near-universal respect. It is "the light above politics", to borrow from the late British philosopher Roger Scruton, "which shines down on the human bustle from a calmer and more exalted sphere".[11]

In New Zealand in 1840 the Treaty of Waitangi was signed with Queen Victoria, not with the government of New Zealand.

> For 78 years we have been, not under the rule of the British, but taking part in the ruling of ourselves, and we know by experience that the foundations of British sovereignty are based upon the eternal principles of liberty, equity and justice.[12]

These are not the words of a British governor but of a Maori leader of 1918. Looking beyond our region, to a forum like the Commonwealth Heads of Government Meeting, reveals this potency to an even more diverse range of cultures – fifty-three nations, all six continents, and 20 per cent of the world's land area.

While modern celebrity appeal undeniably plays a role in the contemporary appreciation of the Crown, the lesson of recent centuries shows, as I touched on at the start, that appreciation follows the institution more than the individual. Or, perhaps ironically, the nature of the individual endures regardless of time. With near-universal admiration, Queen Elizabeth has served for over seven decades by drawing on and extending Queen Victoria's lessons from the previous century – duty, service and acknowledging change. The hereditary example here is not one of ensconced privilege but unbroken continuity – a phenomenon built to last in an age of short-termism. It would be not just Bonner's but Australia's disappointment if we move the goalposts once more.

6

Australia In The World

Australians have achieved so much through our foreign affairs and unique relationships with close neighbours.

From a small British colony to a dynamic regional player, the story of Australia's relationship with the Pacific Islands and Asia – 'relaxed and comfortable', and choosing neither between history and geography – is one of *the* under-appreciated stories of our time.

The republican idea of a regionally reluctant and identity-muddled Australia doesn't quite square with many things about our past – the pragmatic post-federation and Asia-focused efforts of our past political leaders, for example, or even the tough jungle fighting of Australian servicemen in Southeast Asia or the Pacific Islands in World War Two. Nor is it clear how our constitutional monarchy has been so mystifying to the region, especially when a majority of Australians in our main cities are now Asian born.

Regardless, republic advocates see no need to celebrate or revive what has driven these successes, instead putting forward that a republic – with an Australian President

– offers an enhancement of our place in the world. A republic will also improve our commercial reputation in Asia, they say, marshal our foreign policy toward a greater independence, and help mollify any concerns around our perception abroad.

Demographics

Appeals to diversity drive republican claims. It's easy to see Australia at the time of the First Fleet as a monocultural place teeming with white and singular British influence. Many of us, by simply riding a bus, dining out, or even walking down the street, can confirm this is clearly no longer the case. In 2018, according to the Australian Bureau of Statistics, more than half of our population of 25 million was either born overseas or has at least one parent who was.

"At the time our Constitution was put together British heritage had a significant influence on the Australian way of life," noted Sarina Russo – the highly successful Australian businesswoman – at the 1998 Constitutional Convention. "This is no longer true and flies in the face of the great diversity that this nation now possesses".[1]

Australian commentator George Megalogenis adds more recently that, due to our changed demographics, "the south-east corner of Australia is already Eurasian".[2] As such, "Australia's foreign policy needs to shift away from its Anglo European roots," according to one ABC news article, "and engage more positively with the mother countries of foreign-born Australians".[3]

Jieh-Yung Lo – a Chinese-Australian policy adviser, takes this a step further, noting that institutions must reflect demographic change. "If parliament is a reflection of the face of modern Australia," Lo wrote in *Australian Foreign Affairs*, "there should be at least 104 MPs from culturally diverse backgrounds".[4]

To be fair, while not all of these arguments fit squarely into the republican movement's claims, they provide the building blocks for a republic, circling back to an important single and foundational factor – Australian *identity*. If Australia's identity is Asian, or Eurasian, or even *non* British, then a republic offers *the* device to carry out and reflect this change.

It is why republican leaders have tagged the republic to this theme of 'identity'. As long time Australian diplomat Richard Woolcott wrote of Gough Whitlam, "His strong support of an Australian republic was reinforced naturally by his dismissal by the Governor General. But he also saw the need for an Australian republic in the wider context of Australia's identity in the world".[5]

As we know, other figures like Paul Keating saw this in similar terms, tagging Australian identity – a recognition of multiculturalism, equality, Indigenous Australians, and an Australian head of state – as an opportunity to project our 'postcolonial' status abroad.[6]

Commerce

Our overseas business transactions also play a key role in republican persuasions. Britain at the time of the Industrial Revolution – from the 1760s onward – was a major turbine of the global economy. To gain access to British markets was, not just for the colonies but other nations and territories, a significant win for trading prosperity.

The unique blend of Australian merino, developed by John McArthur in the 1790s, eventually outshone American, Spanish and German wool on the international stage. By 1859, "40 million pounds from Australia represented half the raw wool imported into Britain" – no small feat for a once fledgling colony.[7] Over time other Australian agricultural products such as wine, sea elephant oil, silk, tea, dried fruits and fine sand (for glass making) made their inroads into British and other colonial markets.

But as we're now aware, the global commercial picture is much more dispersed. As Asian economic powerhouses have grown so, too, have our commercial ties with northern neighbours. Even with the fallout from COVID-19, Australia's top trading partners today are China followed by Japan, the United States, the Republic of Korea and India.

Republicans note our institutions should reflect this alignment. "With the economic and political balance now shifting to our part of the world," writes former Treasurer Wayne Swan in *Project Republic*, "the idea of an Australian head of state who resides in London seems anachronistic in the extreme".[8] Swan, to be fair, wrote these words in 2013 – a climactic time for the Gillard government's *Asian Century White Paper*. But more recently business leaders like Cameron Clyne – former National Australia Bank CEO – have revived the Asian future argument at expense of the Crown. "You do wonder the degree to which our trading partners look at that symbol," Clyne notes, "and question our real commitment to economic integration with Asia".[9]

Perception

While now out of vogue, it's worth adding that *confusion* over Australia's head of state is another factor that republicans have underlined, at least in past arguments. I've heard many of our diplomats, for example, expressing frustration, and even confessed embarrassment, in having to explain to foreign guests and officials *why* the Queen's portrait hangs on embassy and consular walls.

As former Australian Foreign Minister Gareth Evans notes, "there's definitely a widespread perception around the region that it's very, very odd for a country to have as its Head of State someone living half a world away... it certainly does reinforce the lingering perception that Australia is still a prisoner of its history rather taking advantage of its geography".[10]

Naturally, this leads to other perceptions of a 'stuffy colonialism', tied to a provincial White Australia Policy, which it's claimed still harms closer relations with near-neighbours. It's noted that not just an Australian republic, but a new flag, offers a 'clean break' from the last vestiges of the British Empire – our once guarantor of a White Australia.

British Influence Over Foreign Policy

Two undeniable facts emerge if we look briefly at the history of Australian foreign policy.

The first is that, despite Australia becoming a nation in 1901, Britain retained significant control over our capacity to act independently in world affairs. Britain, it seems, would rarely consult Australia on important regional matters in our early years. Australian historian Judith Brett – in her biography of Australia's second prime minister Alfred Deakin – provides one 1904 example of the British negotiating with the French over the future of New Hebrides (now Vanuatu), and not caring to consult the new federation of Australia. Things were almost formalised but for a deferment in negotiations. "Deakin learned about the postponement from press reports and he was furious," notes Brett.[11] "Here was yet another example of the faraway British government acting without the courtesy of consultation on a matter of direct concern to Australia and New Zealand".

Despite some steady change, our links to Britain were entirely obvious up until World War Two. If Britain was at war with Germany, Menzies famously said in September 1939, then so too was Australia.

The second observation of Australian foreign policy is that it took a long time, even for an energetic new nation, to formally declare independence and take legislative controls back from London. "Independence was offered in 1931 and taken up in late 1942," notes a recent foreign policy commentary of Australia, and it wasn't "until 1940 that Australia established its first diplomatic mission outside of Britain".[12]

Allied to political leadership, these were clear signs of progressive independence. Here again is Gareth Evans, writing in his memoir *The Incorrigible Optimist*:

> Australia did develop, particularly Richard Casey, cordial diplomatic relations with emerging nations of the region; Percy spender not only forged the ANZUS Pact, but his Colombo plan made a very useful contribution to a long term relationship with Asia; John McEwen deserves credit for the 1957 treaty with Japan and the optimism and foresight that went with it; and men like Paul Hasluck, and particularly John Gorton and Harold Holt, had a quite open minded international outlook.[13]

But the residue of British influence, notes Evans, paired with a more conservative worldview, unravels any strides of progressive independence:

> Against all this has to be weighed Menzies's excruciating Anglophilia; maintenance until the late 1960s of the full vigour of the white Australia policy; the stridency of our support for Hendrick Verwoed's apartheid South Africa; the intensity of our antagonism towards China; the totality of our dependence upon the United States; and the ultimate comprehensive misjudgement of our intervention in Vietnam. All this combined to reinforce the image, and the reality, of an Australia largely isolated and irrelevant in its own region, deeply unsure of its identity, utterly pessimistic about its ability to be a force for change in its own right, and in any event wholly unclear about what kind of change it would want to pursue if it could.[14]

Anglosphere Scepticism

Excruciating. Isolated. Irrelevant. Deeply unsure. Evans' critique – especially the invocation of 'Anglophilia' – is a tough indictment upon Australia's achievements and our place in the world.

It's unsurprising, then, that the concept and idea of an Anglosphere – an alliance of like-minded English-speaking nations – receives similar criticism. Despite regaining currency post-Brexit, the Anglosphere is seen as symbolic of outdated thinking in a modern world. Critics of the concept make three main points.

First, they highlight the lack of clarity around economic or trade benefits among Anglosphere nations. Australia, as we know, has over half of its trade tilted toward Asia. The commercial memory of a 1970s Britain turning away from Australia and other Anglosphere nations to Europe is, if not instructive of past pitfalls, also not entirely forgotten.[15]

Second, to a contemporary audience, the Anglosphere inevitably drums up prejudice and jingoism. Deploying the term 'Anglosphere' – especially around inner-city dinner tables – can lead to an awkward defence of some of the rougher edges of empire – counter-insurgency measures, uncomfortable cultural cleavages, anti-insurrection techniques and, to borrow from acclaimed British historian Lawrence James, "a sense of superiority... that frequently bordered on downright xenophobia".[16]

Other civilisations have, of course, engaged in much more brutal forms of territorial expansion. Yet it is the British Empire that remains most salient in our times. This, after all, is the basis for Indian Congress politician Shashi Tharoor's viral Oxford-speech-turned-book *Inglorious Empire: What the British Did to India*. Other empires did bad things, Tharoor concedes, but because the Brits are fresh in living memory they are uniquely liable for cash payments, repatriations and formal apologies like Willy Brandt's knee-dropping penance for Germany.

And third, claims to Anglosphere membership appear to come at the expense of the billions who appear outside of the tent. Granted, the sun never set on the British Empire, and the weight of the Commonwealth – 53 nations, all six continents, and 20 per cent of the world's land area – reveals some serious global appeal. But the Anglosphere appears to exclude places where we are constantly reminded the global future lies – China, large parts of Asia, South America, Russia, and swathes of Europe.

7

Australian Achievements In The World

These republican claims, I admit, mount fair criticisms. Changed demographics, commercial relations, our perception in Asia, and the need for new alliances, all clearly carry some persuasion.

But they don't tell the *full* picture of Australian achievement, or comprehensively explain *why* our institutions, and the Crown, have successfully delivered stability and enhanced our overseas appeal. We're also certainly more diverse. But demographic shifts are not new. And amid difference, Australians will still always seek common ground, especially in a changing nation and shifting geopolitical environment.

Republican proposals also invite many more questions than answers. Is there a need for an Australian President, when Australia's trade and commercial relations with Asia have, year on year, only grown and become more intertwined? How, too, has our perception been so ill-received, or confusing, when we continue to draw thousands of new immigrants from Asia and the rest of the world? Even the offshore 'soft power' appeal of Australia's monarchy – a cultural symbol of tradition, stability and continuity – should invite pause among advocates of a republic.

Demographics – Not Entirely New

Australia, we like to say, is a nation of immigrants. Successive waves of new arrivals came as convicts, many through their own volition, and many more during the gold rush and following World War Two. Over the last decade, in particular, places as diverse as India, the Philippines and Vietnam, have emerged and stayed in the ranks of top ten foreign-born Australians.

A 'southeast Eurasian corner of Australia', therefore, is certainly true today. But if one looks carefully at Australia's mid-nineteenth century gold rush one finds an even more seismic and abrupt change in the demographic makeup of the colonies. In mid-1850s Victoria, for example, nearly a quarter of the rapidly growing population was Chinese-born – something occurring not over decades but in only a few short years.

By itself, and to a modern audience, this seems insignificant. But we can draw from it three important things. First, that our relations with Asia didn't begin with modern instruments like the Colombo Plan or with Whitlam's recognition of China – oft-cited formal starting points of Australia's closer Asian relations.

Second, that our political structures didn't immediately buckle at the sudden change in demographics, requiring an immediate change in the ethnicity of elected officials. And third, it shows us positive lessons around the continual importance of liberal institutions – such as courts, an independent judiciary, and a capable police force – in building social cohesion.

Republicans may feel sceptical, or may even be repelled by British influence in Australian life. But what, after all, did 'British influence' *really* mean, especially when it came to matters of mass migration and social cohesion?

What we find confronts assumptions. "Although colonial governments did use legislation to try to restrict Chinese immigration," according to one Australian historian, "the rule of law in the Australian colonies during the gold rushes by and large defended the Chinese and gave them the same rights as Europeans".[1] "In the early 1850s," half a century *before* the White Australia Policy, "colonial policy in both New South Wales and Victoria supported open immigration".

When the official White Australia Policy eventually emerged, and formally debated as part of the 1901 Immigration Restriction Bill, a range of arguments were accessed that went beyond race and complexion. Some MPs raised wage depression, others expressed solidarity with the Chinese, and others even noted the Bill was actually 'against the traditions of the British Empire'. Context was important, as Judith Brett explains:

> Contemporary Australians regard the White Australia policy as a blot on the nation's past, a product of fear and loathing of a racialised other as the new nation turned away from its region to ensure its place in a white man's world. We need to exercise our historical imagination to understand why Australians at the beginning of the twentieth century could regard it as an expression of high ideals. Yes, boundaries keep outsiders out, but they also enable those inside to co-operate to achieve common goals.[2]

But there's also a much more fundamental point here – that the debate was taking place *within* the institutions of democracy. "Before 19th century pressures from the imperialism of Europe and America," according to Sinologist WJF Jenner, "there was nothing remotely like the notions of positive political freedom or political rights within the public life of society that have developed at the western end of Eurasia over the last 2500 years".[3]

Today, of course, the language of 'political freedom' and 'rights' are such a given that many Australians see them as elasticised – too many rights, one might say, and too little responsibilities. But we need to re-group around the language of political freedom and political rights, not out of nostalgia but because it is necessary for civic renewal, social cohesion and finding common ground.

This is where our constitutional monarchy is much more advantageous than a republic. Modern republicans, for instance, appeal strongly to demographic shifts. But they don't stop there. There exists an over-eagerness to highlight birthplace, complexion, creed, and even privilege and equality, in the republican argument. As the Australian actor John Bell noted, in his 2015 National Republican Lecture, "How can a democratic, egalitarian, multi-cultural and secular society reconcile itself to a Head of State who is, perforce, Anglo-Saxon, Protestant and a member of the House of Windsor?".[4] ARM memes, and other communication material, continually highlights privilege, status and inequality, with any unifying qualities presented by the Crown, or our current constitutional monarchy, tending to be absent.

Prior to modern republicanism, it seems, we paid much less attention to these things. We saw diversity as a source of strength – rallying around shared and colour-blind political structures – and seeing the British monarchy and its legacy as representing ideals and not race, religion or social background.

Matched with economic opportunity, I feel this is a much more appealing legacy to tether ourselves to over republican appeals to difference and division. As Daniel Hannan explains, "The reason why a child of Greek parents in Melbourne is better off than a child of Greek parents in Mytilene has nothing to do with race and everything to do with political structures".[5] Successive waves of Australian migrants have consistently proven this correct.

So what, again, is British influence today? If it is a protection of what one owns, and from scowling mobs, as well as stable politics, under-acknowledging complexion, a sense of fair play and an opportunity for mobility, then I sense these are fundamentals we shouldn't run too far from.

A Monarchy Is Good For Our Economy

Commercial relations are another area where Australia has done exceptionally well. This has happened while we have been a constitutional monarchy, and while Queen Elizabeth has been our Head of State. Year on year trade growth, after all, doesn't seem 'anachronistic'. And nor do Asian counterparts appear confused about Australia's constitutional monarchy.

I suspect this is why many pro-republicans have distanced themselves from this position in recent times. "It is a poor argument to insist that we become a republic in order to be accepted in our region," wrote Hirst in his 1994 *A Republican Manifesto*. "Our business with Asia has already grown immensely even though we have retained our British head of state".[6]

Is A Republic 'Big News' In Asia?

As the Australian political scientist James Curran also notes, it's a stretch arguing that regional capitals wake up "each day fretting about Australia's Constitutional status".[7] Curran – a republican – correctly notes that regional relationships, at least in the short run, can progress regardless of our constitution. "For one thing," he adds, "it didn't seem to hinder Canberra's central role in the creation of APEC, the building of a regional coalition in helping to liberate East Timor, or agreement on any number of bilateral free trade agreements with Asian countries in recent years".[8]

Curran is right. But he doesn't go back far *enough*, especially in underlining that essential but intangible ingredient in foreign affairs – people to people links. Looking back even further than the gold rushes in Australian history, we see that the first Chinese person to come to the colony was Ahuto – a carpenter and free settler arriving in 1803. McArthur's dynamic merino outfit employed Chinese staff. And Mak Sai Ying became a publican of the Parramatta's Lion Inn in 1829.

Again, through a modern lens, this doesn't seem like much. But at the time it no doubt broadcast a message of opportunity in a way that we can't quite ever capture in ABS data, the blogs of international journalists or in formal surveying. "The most important contact between nations," said the Queen after 60 years on the throne, "is usually contact between people".[9]

In the polls we *can* capture, however, it seems, Australians know that a republic will do little to redirect our image abroad. According to a 2014 Lowy Institute Poll, "fifty-five per cent of Australians say that becoming a republic would make no difference to

Australia's standing in the world. Around one in five (19%) say that it would strengthen Australia's standing, and approximately the same number say it would weaken it".[10]

Perception – A Monarchic Appeal?

Modern republicans also tend to forget that monarchy, while maybe passé with the growth in republics worldwide, remains universally recognisable. As Jim Davidson writes:

> The idea of kingship has always had a primitive appeal, the elevated aspects of nobility, grandeur and continuity are yoked to an archetypal version of the family. It is humanity writ large. The trappings of power, if not the substance, means the Windsors have admirers in the United States and even contemporary Russia. You don't have to live in a monarchy to be a monarchist.[11]

So an enchantment with monarchies might remain. But what does this mean for Australian democracy? If we are looking at how Australia is seen in the world, and our image abroad, then there are two things to consider.

The first is that the Asia-Pacific region hosts a quarter of the world's 29 remaining monarchies. Many of these monarchies are likely to see some affinity with Australia's constitutional arrangements. At the same time, it's rather obvious to regional populations that Buckingham Palace no longer signs off on our trade deals, international agreements or any other formal political or diplomatic activities.

Secondly, if any confusion exists, does it justify a wholesale change to a republic? "I have no doubt that there are niceties of the monarchies of Japan, Thailand and Malaysia – not to say of the republics of the region – that we do not fully understand," noted the former High Court Justice Michael Kirby in the early 1990s.[12] Importantly, Kirby adds, "no self-respecting country should abandon its history and institutions out of deference for the misunderstandings of its neighbours".[13]

Foreign Policy And Tradition

Acknowledgement of heritage is not an affront to conducting Australian foreign relations. Indeed, we see this with other nations in our region undertaking much more serious affairs than simple perception management and public diplomacy.

Out of countless countless examples, there's one notable instance that Henry Kissinger explains in the opening to his 2011 book *On China*. During the 1962 Chinese border skirmish with India, Kissinger notes, Mao Tse Tung sat his generals down for a lecture on the Tang Dynasty (618 to 907 AD) and the era of Timurlane (late 1300s). Mao's history briefing, Kissinger notes, wasn't to corral nostalgia but to offer the generals modern strategic lessons to the tactical challenge in front of them – in this case a proposed hit and withdraw by Chinese forces.

Thoroughly modern patriot

"In no other country is it conceivable that a modern leader would initiate a major national undertaking," Kissinger notes, "by invoking strategic principles from a millennium-old event – nor that he could confidently expect his colleagues to understand the significance of his allusions".[14]

My point here is that other nations, in this case a rising superpower, accesses and draws from its history – it doesn't run away from it. So I suspect that as Australians, in acknowledging we have a British past, which shapes and guides our liberal influence in the world, shouldn't conjure *too* much embarrassment. Indeed, as reflected in our range of alliances and commitments to international institutions, Australia's institutional heritage continues to serve as a source of liberal distinction to guide our foreign affairs.

Over time our leaders have, thankfully, respected this balance of both history and geography in pursuing pragmatic political objectives. As Gareth Evans noted earlier, we have made a tremendous amount of regional headway and formed strong regional relationships through the achievements of McEwen, Hasluck, Gorton and Holt. But even before this, prior to World War Two, Australia made strides in Asia, helping build an independent international profile through Barton (Japan), Lyons (Indonesia, China and Japan), Evatt (multilateralism), and Casey (diplomatic relations).

If these examples seem too distant, then the Howard prime ministership illustrates a suitable balance between heritage and geography in more recent times. Howard, as we know, was excoriated for familiar elements Australian republicans hold against Australian monarchists – not taking Asia seriously, denying destiny, for clasping too tightly to the US alliance, and becoming antagonistic toward China. His 1995 reply to Keating's republican proposal was, according to the late journalist Alan Ramsey, "that dreadful. It was facile, contrived, pedestrian and disingenuous... It exposed him more brutally than ever as a leader locked into the past, as a politician of indecision, of no courage, no guile, no ideas, no true understanding of his own country in the 1990s and no feel for the future".[15]

I encourage Australians to actually read Howard's speech. They'll likely find that Ramsey's critique was a tough indictment on Howard's acknowledgement of our history and careful critique of the republican designs at the time.

As we also know, Ramsey's attack also turned out to be not just unfair but wrong. Howard's Asian achievements throughout his eleven-year prime ministership included signing a Free Trade Agreement with China; securing stability and independence with East Timor; growing counter-terrorism ties with Indonesia; renewing diplomatic links with North Korea; bringing Australia into the East Asia Summit; and overseeing the greatest influx of Asian migrants in Australian history. These achievements once again offer the perfect example of balancing history with geography.

An Anglosphere Appeal?

Advocates of the Anglosphere, I concede, need to work harder. And there are three things that can help.

First, they need to plainly point out that the Anglosphere is not about race but an idea. Nelson Mandela, for example, noted it was a deeply held attachment to British ideals that ultimately led to taking on apartheid. Did he agree with every aspect of British foreign conduct? Likely not. But did Mandela see himself fitting into a unique British tradition of liberty? Absolutely.

Second, apply comparisons. Anglosphere advocates need to point to historical alternatives to the Commonwealth and constantly ask critics – 'compared to what?'. Indeed, after looking at historical comparisons, it is clearly much more beneficial to have been settled by the British than French, Portuguese or Spanish empires where, in sum, a respect for the rule of law and its many associated benefits has waned with time.

Furthermore, it can be so simple, as some critics do, dismissing "some modernising benefits" of the Anglosphere without weighing up just how beneficial these elements have been.[16] After all, to possess lineage to the British historian Niall Ferguson's 'killer apps' – "competition, science, property, modern medicine, consumerism and the work ethic" – is much more beneficial than not.[17]

Third, Anglosphere advocates need to better argue where the fusion of ideas and individuals, regardless of political alignment, enables prosperity. Here I do not mean the creative individuals of Silicon Valley tech start-ups but figures like V.S. Naipaul or Chinua Achebe – creative writers that certainly prodded empire but also sensibly respected western and British traditions. The late V.S. Naipaul, for example, wrote, "I couldn't have become the kind of writer I am in Eastern Europe or the Soviet Union or black Africa. I don't think I could have taken my gifts even to India".[18]

For Naipaul, like Mandela, London was not only a place of flourishing but the headquarters to an open access 'universal civilisation'. "I don't imagine my father's parents would have been able to understand the idea," he told the Manhattan Institute in 1991. "So much is contained in it: the idea of the individual, responsibility, choice, the life of the intellect, the idea of vocation and perfectibility and achievement." And Naipaul's attachment to such a worldview, like Mandela's, ultimately had very little to do with complexion.

Most Australians, of course, don't need to go to London to experience this – it is something that we already possess here.

8

Monarchists Old And New

Monarchists, similar to republicans, can be a mixed bunch. In fact, those allied against a republic are arguably *more* diverse – ranging from the 'if it ain't broke' crowd through to die-hard royalists. Over the years I've seen modern monarchists fall broadly into five camps.

First are those that have fierce respect for the Queen and wouldn't have it any other way. These are not the *Women's Weekly* celebrity watchers but those Australians whose respect for the Queen is unwavering, and eager to protect her dignity at every turn. This will extend to King Charles.

Second, there are those who may not be so 'die hard' in their royal respect but who see the dangers of politicising the Governor-General's 'neutral umpire' role. An Australian President, for example, arguing for equality and other social and political priorities, would entangle the position in issues which, as the Australian journalist Fred Pawle argues, could include anything from climate change to sugar taxes – key issues among senior republican lobbyists.[1]

Thoroughly modern patriot

The third group are what I'd call the Constitutionalists – largely legal professionals and academics who see the benefits of drawing Australia back to its legal traditions. These individuals comprise groups like the Sir Samuel Griffith Society.

Fourth are the organised monarchist groups themselves – the Australians for Constitutional Monarchy and the Australian Monarchist League. These groups possess minor distinctions but have been described as like two brands of a very similar car. Both have a wide membership of Australians that, aside from wanting to uphold the Constitution, are proud of our symbols, federation and celebrating tradition. The most obvious distinction is that these Australians are card carrying members – eager enough to fill out membership forms, attend meetings and, where possible, act as spokespersons for their respective organisations.

And finally, there are those that see the republican discussion as a distraction from much more pressing issues. Balancing the budget, for example, or fixing health care or priority education matters.

Reform Monarchism?

Indeed, there are a range of motivations for those who find themselves against an Australian republic. And I hope that underlining this broad alliance does something to contrast the image of a modern monarchist as someone mostly much older, 'flat footed' to modern trends, comfortable with vested interests, and looking to the future through the rear-view mirror.

Indeed, there are prescriptions – let's call them 'gentle prescriptions' – available to modern monarchists rather than simply saying 'no' to a republic. As a monarchist I am naturally careful about putting forward solutions for specific policy problems – those, of course, are issues best left to politicians, experts, think tanks, communities and ultimately voters.

But applying monarchist principles – deferring to accumulated tradition, for example, or exercising national sovereignty, and thinking about our 'soft power' appeal in the world – can serve to improve and renew our democracy. Indeed, a 'monarchist mindset' can offer something toward at least *thinking* about some of our biggest challenges. Here are just a few examples.

Reform To Federation

It's ironic that 'standing up' for the Constitution today immediately postures one for reform. States and territories, envisaged as taking care of health and education, now overlap and entangle with Canberra in terms of funding, service delivery and other responsibilities. Following COVID-19, Australians have been introduced to these overlapping confusions much more acutely.

A more effective federation is the 'index patient' of better government – seeking to limit overlap, duplication, waste and the 'blame game' between the federal and state governments. A working federation goes beyond the confusing sea of performance measures and intergovernmental agreements that we currently have.

But what would a *monarchist* have to say on this issue? I believe a monarchist mindset can help frame and drive federation reform discussions *back* to our Constitution's original wisdom, but in service of *renewing* our federation. Returning responsibilities of health and education to the states, after all, is a Constitutional objective that'll require a significant rebalancing.

Not to be naïve, there are clearly huge hurdles in proper federation reform. The chief obstacle will, ultimately, emerge through taxation and not service delivery. With states and territories collecting only 15 percent of total income tax revenue – a Constitutional responsibility of the federal government – an obvious question will be how to run state and territory education systems and public hospitals without reaching further into people's pockets.

Thinking of this challenge in reverse, GST reform was only possible in the late 1990s because the Howard government helped shed so many unnecessary state taxes – a messy reform that eventually resulted in a cleaner outcome. Federation reform would not wind these reforms back, but ensure a balance that achieves the vision of a working federation limiting overlap, duplication, waste and the 'blame game' between the federal and state governments. Thankfully, there are some bright suggestions out there. And monarchists can help in this discussion.

Asia – Removing Red And Green Tape

Republicans and monarchists share a concern with *how* we are seen in the world. There's a shared emphasis that we haven't done *too* bad a job, at different stages of history, and regardless of what camp one is in. But if we're concerned about our image, then thinking about how themes of tradition, stability and continuity can continue to *appeal* to the region – especially where these things are important – will be critical for current and future policymakers.

A Western rule of law, for example, informs regional arbitration mechanisms, which rest on a strong perception of impartiality. This is one example of an obvious institutional appeal. We also must think hard about our domestic legislative structure, and the litigious nature of modern rule making, while constantly asking how helpful this is to *how* we are seen in the world? The Adani Carmichael mine project, for example, spent 11 years in the approvals process – hardly a winning business broadcast to the region and to a major trading partner.

Another similar analysis, submitted to the federal

government's Environment Protection and Biodiversity Conservation Act 1999 (EPBC Act) review, estimated that the 'lawfare' provision of the EPBC Act has put over $65 billion of investment at risk in Australia by holding up major projects, such as dams, coal mines, and roads, in court.[2] This has amounted to court delays of 10,100 days, or 28 years, since the year 2000.[3] There are many more examples.

Again – these are the practical, legal and policy elements of our system that need fixing. But they can help to improve our regional perception in much more practical ways than our constitutional status. Indeed, they are goals that both republicans and monarchists can work together on.

Careful Sovereignty

Better legislation and federation reform enhance our political system. But they point to something rather obvious – greater sovereignty. Australian parliaments, and not British parliaments, making decisions for Australians, should be something republicans delight in. Indeed, it is what drove early Australian republicans.

Exercising greater national sovereignty does not mean closing up shop and putting up walls to the outside world. But it does, on the sharper ends of policy, mean things like mitigating external interference and thinking hard about immigration reform – key decisions that can't be 'farmed out' to courts, or even an Australian President, but remain for legislators to decide and be held accountable to. After all, what could satisfy republicans more than Australian parliaments – not British parliaments – making key decisions for the Australian people?

On the softer policy edges, careful sovereignty means encouraging home-grown technology and innovation. As the former Dow Chemical Chairman Andrew Liveris explains, an Australian industrial policy can help guide biomedical, farming, advanced materials and other defence capability outcomes.[4] A government playing a sensible 'hands on' role in matching capabilities to opportunities is just an example of where thinking harder about where Australian sovereignty can apply to improve our lives. Especially in unlocking future creative and commercial opportunities.

Reignite CHOGM

One other creative way that it might apply is thinking about what Australian sovereignty can offer to international institutions and protecting human dignity.

In Australia we have done tremendously well to 'walk the talk' when it comes to protecting human rights. But, internationally, it's fair to say projecting or even advancing human rights tends not to get the same coverage as it has in previous decades. There is an element of skepticism toward the international human rights machinery, which is understandable when nations like Cuba, China and Iran chair human rights councils, and Israel is the only nation appearing in breach of various conventions and agreements.

But there's a more optimistic case to be made when we examine an institution like the Commonwealth Heads of Government Meeting (CHOGM). Back in the late 1990s and early 2000s, we forget that it was leaders like John Howard and South Africa's Thabo Mbeki – a very unlikely press conference duo – exerting the most acute political pressure on the late Zimbabwean President Robert Mugabe.

Their mechanism? The Commonwealth Ministerial Action Group or 'CMAG' which, according to former CHOGM head Don McKinnon, is a diplomatic group all CHOGM leaders would desperately seek to avoid expulsion from. "No country likes to be thrown out or suspended, or even chastised by members of an organisation they have willingly joined," explains McKinnon.[5] "A CMAG might not always be the best possible mechanism," he adds realistically. "But I do believe that globally it's the best to date".[6]

Through our connection to the Crown, this puts us in unique company – like-minded nations, which look *very* different on face value, coming together and applying pressure on illiberal governments and regimes. Importantly, this isn't because our shared institutions are *Anglo*, or 'white', but because they are fundamentally built on the idea of *liberty*.

CHOGM also stands up for issues like environmental conservation, electoral transparency and support, youth skills and employment, and building democratic trust. These are things Australians can authentically support and, again, places us in an exclusive orbit of friends – one that we'll do well to stay within and consider boosting our contribution to.

Like many other democratic enhancements not covered here, a monarchist mindset can help to improve our democracy in the twenty-first century. We don't have to completely run from our past, and our constitutional monarchy, to continue on our path to democratic improvement.

Conclusion

A Time For Patriots

At the start of this short book, I carefully placed a chapter on the future. Readers will recall that it spoke of how our institutions lay the ground for 'our vision' – the scaffolding upon which we can continue to attempt to prosper and grow.

In the intervening pages I hope to have shown that our institutions have been shaped by Britain, which inextricably includes the British Monarchy. These haven't been lock-stock and wholesale British transplants – distinctive Australian features of egalitarianism, pragmatism, local leadership and other home-grown events have, over time, resulted in unique and organic democratic features. These elements have also turned a *British* monarchy into an *Australian* monarchy.

I am proud of Australia. This is something instinctive that has grown with time, reading voraciously and steadily becoming ever-grateful for two things – good people and sound institutions. 'Top down' and 'bottom up'. We are a quietly tenacious nation, buoyed by rounds of immigrants that have accepted and subscribed to the ideals commended upon them by generations of Australians.

We can continue to be a stable, prosperous and liberal democracy. But I firmly believe this – it can only be continued over the long-term by remaining a constitutional monarchy.

I say this not to be divisive, or to issue a damning ultimatum to fellow Australians. But an Australian republic, with its grand designs on the Constitution, and the rules it entangles the Governor-General, will lead us towards logjam, political overreach and instability. At a time when democratic decline, and even scepticism, is emerging as a defining feature of our age then we should be careful about the downward slide a republic – a problem looking for a solution – can pull us toward.

As Australians, this is our time to not just say 'no' to a republic but think hard of the challenges of our days, and how our democratic system can resolve, renew and continue to enable us in the twenty-first century. This is a task not just for 'monarchists' or 'republicans'. Indeed, it is our central challenge as modern patriots.

Endnotes

A SHORT NOTE ON THE FUTURE

1 Malcolm Turnbull, *The Reluctant Republic*, Hardie Grant Books, 20 April 2020, Kindle Edition.

2 Laura Tingle, *Great Expectations: Government, Entitlement and an Angry Nation*, Black Inc, Melbourne, 2012, 63.

PREFACE

1 Andrew Bacevich, 'Best Intentions: An Appreciation of Graham Greene', *World Affairs*, Summer 2009.

2 Tim Soutphommasane, 'Gangnam points to our future', *Sydney Morning Herald*, 8 October 2012.

1 A LAZY COSMOPOLITAN

1 Simon Barnes, 'Maro Itoje is a national hero for our time', *The Spectator*, 2 November 2019.

2 John Howard, 'Address to the Australian Liberal Students Federation', *PM Transcripts*, Sydney University, 8 July 2020.

3 Paul Keating, 'An Australian Republic – The Way Forward', *Australian Politics*, 7 June 1995.

2 SOMETHING TO BE PROUD OF

1 Joseph Banks in G Arnold Wood, *The Voyage of the Endeavour (1926)*, Project Gutenberg Australia, June 2016, Online resource.

2 See WP Morrell (ed), *Sir Joseph Banks in New Zealand*, A. H. & A. W. Reed, Wellington, 1958, 24.

3 Thomas Barlow, *The Australian Miracle*, Pan Macmillan, Sydney, 2006, 77.

4 Grace Karskens, *The Colony: A History of Early Sydney*, Allen & Unwin, Sydney, 2009, 126.

5 Niall Ferguson, *Empire: How Britain Made the Modern World*, Penguin, Camberwell, 2003, 104.

6 This is Brian Fletcher's assessment of LL Robson, Manning Clark and A.G.L Shaw's independent research reaching "broadly similar conclusions" that crime for convicts was "less a result of necessity than of choice". See Brian Fletcher, 'Australia's Convict Origins', *History Today*, Volume: 42 Issue: 10, 1992, 39-43.

7 Charles Darwin, *The Voyage of the Beagle (1839)*, Project Gutenberg, 24 June 2013, Online resource.

8 Geoffrey Dutton, *The Squatters*, Currey O'Neil, Australia, 1985, 4.

9 George Orwell, *Why I Write*, Penguin Books, 2004, 32.

10 This comment was reported in *The Australian* at the time. See Erica Izett, 'Breaking New Ground: Early Australian Ethnography in Colonial Women's Writing', The University of Western Australia, Doctoral Thesis, 2014.

11 David Flint, 'They Did Not Come Alone', *The Crowned Republic*, 14 May 2010.

12 Keith Windschuttle, 'Vilifying Australia', *Quadrant*, September 2005, Earle Page Memorial Oration, Delivered at Parliament House, Sydney, 22 June 2005.

13 Daniel Hannan, *Inventing Freedom: How the English-Speaking Peoples Made the Modern World*, HarperCollins, 2013, Kindle Edition.

14 Bob Hawke, 'Speech By The Prime Minister Citizenship Ceremony Preston', *PM Transcripts*, 19 July 1988.

15 Daniel Deniehy, 'The Bunyip Aristocracy', 1853. Available at *Independent Australia*, 7 February 2011, Online resource.

16 Ian McAllister, *The Australian Voter*, UNSW Press, Sydney, 2011, 27.

17   Helen Irving, *Five Things to Know About the Australian Constitution*, Cambridge University Press, 2004, 47.

18   Dutton, *The Squatters*, 5.

19   Nick Cater, *The Lucky Culture*, HarperCollins, 2013, Kindle Edition.

20   Thomas Barlow, 'The Role of National Character in Australia's Prosperity', *Quadrant*, April 2013, 20.

21   Samuel Smiles, *Self Help (1859)*, Project Gutenberg, 28 December 2014, Online resource.

22   Barlow, *Australian Miracle*, 96-97.

23   Miles Franklin, *My Brilliant Career (1901)*, Project Gutenberg Australia, June 2020, Online resource.

24   John Hirst, 'Federation: Destiny and Identity', Senate Occasional Lecture, 21 July 2000.

25   Although there are many Australian political leaders to have played a part in federation, I have selected Barton, Parkes and Reid as arguably the most important and consequential.

26   Barton's words taken from Geoffrey Bolton, *Edmund Barton*, Allen & Unwin, 2000, Kindle Edition.

27   AW Martin, 'Parkes, Sir Henry (1815–1896)', *Australian Dictionary of Biography*, Volume 5, Melbourne University Press.

28   Hirst, 'Federation: Destiny and Identity'.

29   WC McGinn, 'Biography of George Houston Reid', *Australian Dictionary of Biography*, Melbourne, 1998.

30   Ibid.

31   Bolton, *Edmund Barton*.

3 TOO BROAD A CHURCH: WHAT'S DRIVING AN AUSSIE REPUBLIC?

1   Bob Brown in *Australian Financial Review*, 1 September 1997.

2   Benjamin T Jones, *This Time: Australia's Republican Past and*

Future, Black Inc. Redback, 24 January 2018, Kindle Edition.

3   John Dunmore Lang, 'To the electors of the city of Sydney', 2 September 1851 in David Headon and Elizabeth Perkins (eds), *Our First Republicans*, The Federation Press, Annandale, 1998, 32.

4   John Hirst, *Freedom on The Fatal Shore: Australia's First Colony*, Black Inc, Melbourne, 2008, 440.

5   Turnbull, *The Reluctant Republic*.

6   Geoffrey Dutton in James Curran and Stewart Ward, *The Unknown Nation: Australia After Empire*, Melbourne University Press, 2010, 85.

7   Turnbull, *The Reluctant Republic*.

8   Ibid.

9   Jones, *This Time: Australia's Republican Past and Future*.

10 Australian Republic Movement, 'Frequently Asked Questions', Online resource.

4   A MONARCHIST'S RESPONSE

1   *Instructions for American Servicemen in Australia*, United States Army, Washington DC, 1942, 37-38.

2   The quotes in this section are taken from Paul Hasluck, *The office of Governor-General*, Melbourne University Press, Carlton, Victoria, 1979.

3   Richard McGarvie, *Democracy: Choosing Australia's Republic*, Melbourne University Press, 1999, 23.

4   Donald Markwell, 'The Office of Governor-General', Melbourne University Law Review, 3; (2015) 38(3) Melbourne University Law Review 1098.

5   Hasluck, *The Office of Governor-General*.

6   John Howard in 'Radio interview: Howard Defends Sir John Kerr', *Australian Politics*, 3 November 1999.

7   Jim Davidson, 'The lost option', *Griffith Review*, Number 36, 26 April 2012.

8   Ibid.

9   Ibid.

10 Tony Abbott, *The Minimal Monarchy*, Wakefield Press, Sydney, 1995, 120.

11 Francis Fukuyama, 'The Last English Civil War', *Daedus American Academy of Arts and Sciences*, Winter 2018, 15.

12 Stephanie Forrest, 'Our English Inheritance', *Institute of Public Affairs*, 1 August 2018.

5   INDIGENOUS AUSTRALIANS AND THE MONARCHY'S PROMISE

1   Neville Bonner cited in Tony Abbott, '2010 Neville Bonner Oration', Australians For Constitutional Monarchy, 27 November 2010.

2   Mark McKenna, 'A symbolic life', *Griffith Review*, Edition 9, August 2006.

3   Felicity Caldwell, 'Noel Pearson calls for republic delay until Indigenous vote can be held', *Sydney Morning Herald*, 10 November 2017.

4   Malcolm Turnbull, 'Response to Referendum Council's report on Constitutional Recognition', 26 October 2017, Online resource.

5   David Hill, *The Special Relationship: Australia and the Monarchy*, Penguin Random House, North Sydney, 2016, 375.

6   Ibid, 7.

7   'Foreword from Co-Chairs', Final Report of the Referendum Council, 17 August 2018.

8   David Kemp, *Land of Dreams: How Australians Won Their Freedom 1788 – 1860*, Melbourne University Press, Carlton, 2018, 16.

9   Sean Jacobs, 'Neville Bonner: A legacy for young Australians', *Policy*, Vol 29 no 4, Summer 2013-14, 49.

10 James Cook, 'Cook's Journal Daily Entries' (30 April 1770), *National Library of Australia*.

11 William Shawcross, 'The genius of monarchy', *The Spectator*, 22 May 2018.

12 Hannan, *Inventing Freedom*.

6 AUSTRALIA IN THE WORLD

1 Sarina Russo, Constitutional Convention 1998 – Day 6 – Hansard, 9 February 1998, 558.

2 Jim Jirik and Beverley O'Connor, 'George Megalogenis says Australia must embrace Eurasian future', *Australian Broadcasting Corporation*, 18 October 2017.

3 Ibid.

4 Jieh-Yung Lo, 'Response To George Megalogenis' "The Changing Face Of Australia"', *Australian Foreign Affairs*, October 2017.

5 Richard Woolcott, 'Whitlam on the world stage: Courage, vision and wit', *Lowy Institute*, 28 October 2014.

6 Isabella Ostini, 'Foreign policy with an Australian accent', *Australian Foreign Affairs*, May 2019.

7 W David McIntyre, *Colonies into Commonwealth*, Blanford Press, London, 1974, 55.

8 Wayne Swan in Mark McKenna and Benjamin Jones (eds), *Project Republic: Plans and Arguments for a New Australia*, Black Inc, 22 May 2013, Kindle Edition.

9 Patrick Durkin, 'Australian republic 'economically important' say business leaders', *Australian Financial Review*, 21 January 2019.

10 Gareth Evans in 'Interview with Gareth Evans, ex-Australian Foreign Minister', *Your Commonwealth*, 1 May 2012.

11 Judith Brett, *The Enigmatic Mr Deakin*, Text Publishing, 14 August 2017, Kindle Edition.

12 Adil Cader, 'What The History Of Australian Independence

Can Tell Us About Britain's Journey Ahead', *Oxpol*, 15 January 2020.

13 Gareth Evans, *Incorrigible Optimist*, Melbourne University Publishing, Melbourne, 2017, 102.

14 Ibid.

15 Ben Wellings, 'Brexit and Australia: free trade, the Anglosphere and Anglo-Scepticism', *UK in a Changing Europe*, 26 January 2019.

16 Lawrence James, *The Rise and Fall of the British Empire*, Abacus, London, 1994, xiv.

7 AUSTRALIAN ACHIEVEMENTS IN THE WORLD

1 Keith Windschuttle, *The White Australia Policy: Race and Shame in the Australian History Wars*, Macleay Press, Sydney, 2001, 172.

2 Brett, *The Enigmatic Mr Deakin*.

3 WJF Jenner, 'China and Freedom', in David Kelly and Anthony Reid (eds), *Asian Freedoms: The Idea of Freedom in East and Southeast Asia*, Cambridge University Press, Melbourne, 1998, 75.

4 John Bell, 2015 National Republican Lecture, *Australian Republic Movement*, 15 November 2015.

5 Nick Cater, 'Like it or not, national character owes much to the mother country', *The Australian*, 14 February 2014.

6 John Hirst, *A republican manifesto*, Oxford University Press, Melbourne, 1996, 105.

7 James Curran, 'Rhetorical arthritis won't sell an Australian republic', *Lowy Institute*, 11 August 2017.

8 Ibid.

9 Don McKinnon, *In the Ring: A Commonwealth Memoir*, Elliott and Thompson, London, 2013, 22.

10 Alex Oliver, 'Lowy Institute Poll 2014', *Lowy Institute*, 2 June 2014.

11 Jim Davidson, 'The lost option'.

12 Michael Kirby, 'A defence of the constitutional monarchy', *Quadrant*, September 1993, 30-35.

13 Ibid.

14 Henry Kissinger, *On China*, Allen Lane, Maryborough, Victoria, 2011, 2.

15 Tony Abbott, *How to win the constitutional war and give both sides what they want*, Australians for Constitutional Monarchy/ Wakefield Press, Sydney, 1997, 45.

16 Allan Patience, 'Australia's involvement in an 'Anglosphere' is the delusion of a golden age that never existed', *The Conversation*, 24 May 2017.

17 Niall Ferguson, 'The 6 killer apps of prosperity', *TED*, July 2011.

18 VS Naipaul, 'Our Universal Civilization', *City Journal*, Summer 1991.

8 MONARCHISTS OLD AND NEW

1 Fred Pawle, 'The PC President', *Menzies Research Centre*, 28 August 2018.

2 Cian Hussey, '445% Increase In Federal Environmental Regulation Since 2000', *Institute of Public Affairs*, 24 April 2020.

3 Ibid.

4 Andrew Liveris, 'Leadership in the 21st Century: How to respond to increasing volatility and the new tectonic trends defining our world', National Press Club Address, *Australian Broadcasting Corporation*, 16 September 2020.

5 Don McKinnon, *In the Ring*, 71.

6 Ibid, 50.

www.ingramcontent.com/pod-product-compliance
Lightning Source LLC
Chambersburg PA
CBHW030142170426
43199CB00008B/171